It was Mark who helped me quickly realize that the strengths that helped me earn my promotion were not the same strengths that would enable me to excel in it. I was an Exhausted Hero, and to be frank, no one really likes working for an Exhausted Hero. Mark helped me improve my leadership skills through the tools in this great book.

—HEIDI COOLEY

Head of Global Marketing, Crocs

Both aspirational and practical, Rescuing the Corporate Exhausted Hero *offers a better way of doing business by leveraging employee expertise rather than revering the act of running ourselves into the ground.*

—KATY CRAIG

Creative Navigator, Pavo Leadership

Rescuing the Corporate Exhausted Hero *is a wonderful book packed with actionable advice for a leader to rescue themselves and their teams. Mark is insightful and inspiring! Once you read this book, you will understand how to identify your Exhausted Heroes and create a culture where they can thrive, versus fail and ultimately quit you.*

—KATHLEEN QUINN VOTAW

Chief Executive Officer, TalenTrust

RESCUING THE CORPORATE EXHAUSTED HERO

MARK HEYDT

RESCUING THE CORPORATE EXHAUSTED HERO

A LEADERSHIP GAME PLAN TO ACHIEVE IT ALL
WITHOUT DOING IT ALL

Published by Advantage, Charleston, South Carolina.
Member of Advantage Media Group.

ADVANTAGE is a registered trademark, and the Advantage colophon is a trademark of Advantage Media Group, Inc.

Printed in the United States of America.

10 9 8 7 6 5 4 3 2 1

ISBN: 978-1-64225-139-5
LCCN: 2020912456

Cover design by David Taylor.
Layout design by Megan Elger.

This publication is designed to provide accurate and authoritative information in regard to the subject matter covered. It is sold with the understanding that the publisher is not engaged in rendering legal, accounting, or other professional services. If legal advice or other expert assistance is required, the services of a competent professional person should be sought.

Advantage Media Group is proud to be a part of the Tree Neutral® program. Tree Neutral offsets the number of trees consumed in the production and printing of this book by taking proactive steps such as planting trees in direct proportion to the number of trees used to print books. To learn more about Tree Neutral, please visit **www.treeneutral.com**.

Advantage Media Group is a publisher of business, self-improvement, and professional development books and online learning. We help entrepreneurs, business leaders, and professionals share their Stories, Passion, and Knowledge to help others Learn & Grow. Do you have a manuscript or book idea that you would like us to consider for publishing? Please visit **advantagefamily.com** or call **1.866.775.1696**.

CONTENTS

WE IN CORPORATE AMERICA CAN DO BETTER

Every day across corporate America, highly talented employees are hitting the wall, arriving at a point in their career where their only options are to grit their teeth and try to hang on until retirement—or to quit. Burnout is rampant, a plague in every company at all levels, from the C-suite to the frontline managers in the field. The erosion it's causing in morale is destructive and expensive, and it produces a host of other problems in our personal and professional lives.

I'm not talking about simply being tired. We all work hard, and most of us are willing to put in the extra energy to get a project across the finish line. Being tired is temporary and can be resolved by taking a break or vacation. Burnout isn't about being tired; it's about being exhausted. Exhaustion comes when you are always working hard but not feeling as though you're being productive or moving anything forward. Exhaustion comes with too many sleepless nights and regularly sacrificing family time, your health, or your days off to keep up with the never-ending demands of your job. Exhaustion leads to burnout for many leaders after too many all-nighters, followed by long days at the office. These leaders continue to take on more responsibilities while trying to keep up their teams' energy and enthusiasm as their own morale sinks. But even the most optimistic leader will collapse under this weight eventually, and burnout will be the inevitable outcome.

It doesn't have to be this way.

No matter how demanding the work may be, we have many more choices to avoid burnout than most of us realize. But because burnout is so overwhelming, most of us feel paralyzed and need help finding a better way. Worst of all, as we struggle, we neglect our personal development, and we fail to keep the needed focus on our own well-being.

One extreme but all-too-common example: Ryan was a middle manager at a multibillion-dollar global manufacturing company. While managing a team of five direct reports, he also maintained his own individual-contributor workload by managing a key account. As fires ignited across his department, he would jump in to put them out, swooping in like Superman to save the day for his team. But we humans aren't built to take on this kind of superhero role, and his blood pressure was through the roof. His doctor had to put him on hypertension medications and recommended he take it easier. That wasn't going to happen—the stress just didn't let up—and eventually Ryan had to tell his boss, "I don't think I can do this anymore. I'm afraid I've got to find another job."

The boss, to her credit, realized how serious the situation was—for Ryan's health, development, and career, as well as for the success of his team and their contribution to the company. With all that in mind, she told him, "Let's step back. We see you as high potential, as somebody who can think critically and who can do amazing work as an expert. Quitting is not the answer. Let's get you to a place where you can have your team help you. Let's get you help in developing new skills and finding balance in your work."

Mentally, Ryan was already halfway out the door. But with this intervention, his boss was able to save him from the brink of total burnout. He was lucky his boss recognized the opportunity. She brought in an executive coach—me—to help Ryan.

I worked with Ryan for six months. We used the tools I'll describe later in this book to assess and address the challenges that contributed to his burnout. Slowly, we started walking him back from some of those traps that he was stepping into, which were causing him to overload himself and get overwhelmed. He learned the critical skill of how to delegate with his team. We taught him that when a challenge or a problem happened within the business, he didn't have to take it all on his shoulders.

Thanks to that intervention, not only was he able to help solve new problems without experiencing burnout, but he was finally able to focus on the development of his own team. He became a manager more focused on being strategic, able to spend his time working on the big picture and on big-ticket items, rather than on putting out all the little fires. His hero status became less reactive as he became a more proactive leadership hero.

Today, Ryan is thriving and still with the company—and within six months of our having worked together to bring him back from the brink, he was promoted.

We can and must do better for our people and ourselves than simply surrendering to burnout. We can save Exhausted Heroes like

Ryan. And if you're an Exhausted Hero yourself, there's so much hope—and this book will help you understand how to fight back.

Some Exhausted Heroes are waiting for the company to solve their exhaustion issues. And sometimes the company can help, through restructuring and additional resources. But the majority of the time, the Exhausted Heroes themselves can learn to make better choices and have clearer intentions to avoid exhaustion.

Maybe you're reading this book because

- you're an Exhausted Hero who knows you can become a better leader;

- you're an Exhausted Hero who's looking for a new job because you can't take it anymore;

- the constructive feedback keeps coming, but you're already too drained to figure out how;

- the high-potential talent in your organization is leaving you in droves;

- your team isn't working on full throttle, expectations are upside down, and you are scared that you'll lose great people; or

- you're an executive who wants your managers to become strategic in all that they do.

No matter *why* you picked up the book, I hope it allows you to create an actionable Game Plan, helping you carve out a meaningful and fulfilling role in corporate America.

IMPORTANT DISCLAIMER

Executive coaching is a personal and confidential engagement. It is important that the discussions between a coach and a client are created in a space of trust and integrity. In respecting the trust and integrity of the coaching process, all anecdotal examples in this book have been masked with new names and other slightly altered information to protect my coaching clients' identities and privacy. I did reach out to clients for permission to use their experiences if their experiences were mentioned in extreme detail. I'm grateful for their generous permission to use their stories to help rescue other Exhausted Heroes via this book.

CHAPTER 1

ARE YOU AN EXHAUSTED HERO?

It's a Monday morning in the HR department of a *Fortune* 500 company, and there's an anxious buzz on the executive floor. The COO, who usually walks with deliberate confidence, hurries nervously into the chief HR officer's office and shuts the door. Five minutes later, the CEO flies by to join them. A few minutes later, the compensation manager is called in. What's happened?

Yep—another high-potential leader has given her notice and left the building. This time it's Amanda, the only female vice president in the large operations division. Losing Amanda is a shock to the senior leadership team, because she was knee-deep in rolling out a new process intended to save the organization millions in expenses while increasing revenues by 25 percent over the next two years.

Throughout the past six years—ever since she joined the company as a frontline manager—Amanda has been driven and passionate in representing the business. Few employees demonstrated higher potential than Amanda. With all she had going for her, why would she simply quit and effectively torpedo her own career?

In the emergency meeting that followed Amanda's departure, the CEO and COO comment about Amanda's bright future with the company. Stunned by her resignation, they insist to one another that they can't let her "throw it all away."

The initial shock is huge, but even more concerning for these executives is how the company will backfill her vital role and maintain the momentum she brought to her projects. Only Amanda knows the new cost-saving process. Without her, the whole strategy—just promised to the board of directors—may go down in flames.

The CEO and COO ask the chief human resources officer, "How do we change Amanda's mind?" They discuss the need to avoid the high cost of turnover and the typical six-month ramp-up for any new employee. Then they all turn to the compensation manager and ask about Amanda's compensation: "How much is she making? How much more can we give her? Will she stay for that amount?"

While the C-suite deliberates, two blocks from the office in a small coffee shop, Amanda is ordering herself a latte and a slice of chocolate cake. She tells the cashier, "I deserve this today!" After receiving her order, she sits down, overwhelmed with both exhaustion and relief. Amanda's perspective is quite different from the confusion and panic happening back at the office with her senior leaders. Yes, she is passionate and proud about the work she has been doing at the company. But she is just plain exhausted. Burned out!

Over the past few months, she had asked for help but didn't get it. She had asked for an additional head count to help complete her project, but that request was denied. She had asked for an extension to some deadlines and was told that wasn't possible. The CEO even provided her with feedback two months previously, saying that she needed to be "more strategic." After completing her long list of individual-contributor tasks, she rarely had the time or energy to be the strategic leader she was expected to be. Her boss, the COO, counseled her to just "hang in there," as now wasn't the time for him to fight for head count or to put his own career on the line by delaying the project. And despite her best efforts on their behalf, her team was becoming increasingly frustrated with the tight turn-arounds and high expectations, causing a key team member to resign recently. Would others soon follow suit?

Amanda knew she'd been personally out of balance. She was typically the first to get in to the office and the last to leave. She juggled keeping her team happy, her bosses happy, and her inbox down. She regularly skipped lunch, unless she was in a meeting where lunch was ordered for her. She had all but given up on her workout routine. She hadn't taken a vacation day all year, and she hadn't slept well in a long time. Most nights, after struggling to fall asleep, she'd wake after a few hours, already worrying about the day ahead of her.

Back in the CHRO's office, what the senior leaders don't realize is that Amanda is an Exhausted Hero. She is the typical do-it-all leader who struggles to balance all the priorities of leading the business, managing the team, and executing the details. Most struggle trying to take it all on to save the business, until they're overwhelmed and worn down—an Exhausted Hero.

We find Exhausted Heroes everywhere in corporate America—and their ranks are growing. Faced with burnout and little understanding from senior leadership, many Exhausted Heroes make the lifesaving decision to leave.

> **Most struggle trying to take it all on to save the business, until they're overwhelmed and worn down—an Exhausted Hero.**

After what felt like months of begging for help, Amanda has reached the point of no return. She's hung on as long as she could but finally has given up on her dream of a future with the company. Now, as she sits in the coffee shop, relieved at having quit, she's not worrying about finding another job. She's just content to be having a piece of cake.

The executives, meanwhile, are spinning their wheels, designing a counteroffer for Amanda. What they don't know is that there's not enough money in the world to get her to come back. Every option they discuss is too little, too late. She's gone for good.

As Amanda finishes her cake, a single, anxious thought crosses her mind. She reflects on her recent experiences and realizes she doesn't know *what exactly* she could have done differently. What if she gets a new job and falls into the same patterns? How is she going to find the balance she needs?

How could she—and her senior leadership—have done things differently, to avoid her becoming an Exhausted Hero?

DEFINING THE EXHAUSTED HERO

Before we explore what Amanda and her senior leadership team could've done differently, let's lay out a working definition of the Exhausted Hero, a concept we'll return to regularly throughout the book.

After years of coaching Exhausted Heroes and working with senior leadership in companies of all sizes, here's the best definition I've come up with thus far: an Exhausted Hero tries to balance owning individual-contributor work and managing a team, while taking a larger leadership role in setting a vision for the team, influencing progress, and leading change.

Exhausted Heroes drive results, are technical experts, manage teams, manage resources, manage projects, set the vision for the team, and influence change, all while leading and coaching others. It is exhausting just reading that laundry list of expected responsibilities. Sadly, Exhausted Heroes may manage to juggle all of these responsibilities for a while. But they probably can't manage to do any of them very well. Eventually they will lose the desire to try or will simply walk away from these impossible expectations.

Let me share with you an example of Exhausted Hero burnout, from my early days in retail.

Years ago, when I was a corporate retail employee, I attended a new store opening in my neighborhood as a customer. I had gotten to know the store manager well, as he previously had led another store in town. He was very capable, and I was excited to share with him the excitement of a beautiful new store.

When I arrived, I found my friend the store manager hiding in the corner—literally. Meanwhile, his boss, the regional vice president, was running around the store doing everything at once. One minute he was on the microphone conducting a raffle while barking out orders to the cashiers up front; the next moment, he was stocking shelves.

This regional vice president was a classic Exhausted Hero. As a leader, he was responsible for the performance of over one hundred stores across ten states. He was accountable for implementing new strategic directives from the corporate office and ensuring all processes were followed correctly. He was responsible for coaching the management teams and driving change across his region. But this Exhausted Hero was known as a workaholic who often worked seven days a week and spent many hours working in the stores. In his exhaustion, he became very short with his team and, in his frustration, would lose patience, roll up his sleeves, and jump into their roles to fix the issues he saw himself.

Now, at the new store opening event, this Exhausted Hero was not only working below his pay grade, but he was literally pushing his direct report out of the way. It wasn't surprising that the direct report was paralyzed; who wouldn't have been? Now had that vice president been a Strategic Manager, he would have asked the manager, "What do you need most from me today? Stocking shelves? No problem! Providing encouragement to the team? No problem."

Instead, he was driving results and managing the team on his own, working as a functional expert while trying to lead change. Yes, the VP was juggling all of these roles at once, but he wasn't doing any of them well. And his most important role—which was to coach his direct report to implement the strategy for the new store—was completely lost! Far from helping the team, this Exhausted Hero was contributing to its stress, burnout, and even turnover.

Exhausted Hero Examples:

- The CEO who continues to pull his own reports every day

- The restaurant manager who starts grilling burgers while the front of the restaurant is disgustingly dirty

- The football coach who also plays the scout team quarterback in practice

- The marketing director who attends every photo shoot and positions the shots

- Write your example here:

  _____

HOW DO WE BECOME EXHAUSTED HEROES?

An Exhausted Hero is usually created as an individual contributor moves up the career ladder, gaining more and more responsibilities, placing greater demand and expectations on their plate. Most start as a Taskmaster, getting tasks done and continuously getting more responsibility. Then they are elevated to Rockstar status as the technical or functional expert. They continue to gain more tasks and projects. These Rockstars get promoted to manager but maintain individual-contributor work while managing the complexities of running a team. Then, their boss asks them to be strategic and build the future plan while also managing their team and maintaining an individual contributor's workload.

The person who eventually becomes an Exhausted Hero is usually someone who's previously excelled, and the job just keeps growing. Their supervisor notices and gives them more responsibility. Then, at some point, as the responsibilities add up and their team grows, a tipping point is reached, and their personal growth stalls—due to lack of support or direction from leadership, lack of understanding on how to develop on their part, or both—and they're unable to move on from being *just* a Rockstar. They'll keep on doing double duty as manager and Rockstar, but it's a struggle—and the struggle will continue. If they don't develop into a Strategic Manager, they risk burnout.

We all know this person. We may in fact *be* this person, struggling to balance it all. Always playing firefighter and feeling like the work is out of control, this leader feels the pressure to be strategic, along with meeting demands to deliver results, while feeling the guilt of being a less-than-effective people manager.

Symptoms include the following:

- Being the first person to work and the last one to leave

- Gaining recognition for getting things accomplished—then being "rewarded" with more projects

- Running from meeting to meeting but never feeling like they are accomplishing anything

- In their office, straining to get control of their overflowing inbox while trying to dodge an endless parade of employees coming to them with questions

The reason these people come in early and leave late is that is the only time they are not bothered and can get their work done. Because they are the ones whom senior leaders can count on to complete the most challenging projects, their to-do pile just keeps growing. Is it any surprise that these people feel overwhelmed or that they can't see there's another, better way?

Yes, there are inevitably going to be times in your professional life that you'll be called upon to perform like an Exhausted Hero. The quarterly report is due tomorrow. The big sales meeting is next week. The CEO just came asking for a report for the board meeting. All of these are examples of short-term fires of high importance that you may be asked to dive into. And there are projects your team will need you to help them with, which require you to perform double duty. In cases like these, being an Exhausted Hero for a short period of time can be a good thing, garnering you the

But if you are planning on sustaining the Exhausted Hero role for a substantial period of time, you are asking for an out-of-balance, exhausted life in which you're courting mediocrity, burnout, and career suicide.

respect of higher-ups and of your team. But if you are planning on sustaining the Exhausted Hero role for a substantial period of time, you are asking for an out-of-balance, exhausted life in which you're courting mediocrity, burnout, and career suicide.

THE RISKS OF THE EXHAUSTED HERO

For those senior leaders reading this who are wondering why your high-potential talent is leaving, it may be because you are trapping them in an exhausting role. By giving them too little management training, saddling them with downsized teams, and failing to provide them with adequate development and guidance, you've put them in the untenable position of having to triage their own roles on the fly, neglecting some parts of their responsibilities and prioritizing others, as the demands on them mount.

An Exhausted Hero is not a sustainable role, but it is a role a majority of managers have experienced at some point in their careers. And it comes with a few big risks.

Double Duty Means Mediocrity, Not Strategy

By trying to do it all, the Exhausted Hero is kept too busy to identify or plan for approaching challenges. This lack of planning or vision forward means they're continuously reacting to crises. If crisis management becomes the day-to-day norm, the leader will burn out fast, their team will become disengaged, and deliverables will fall through the cracks.

Trying to be and do everything means that everything gets done at a mediocre level. The overwhelmed feeling comes from trying to do it all and being the hero for all. But trying to be an executor in the now while also planning the strategy for the future is a challenging balance to achieve. If you're trying to do this while managing a team, are you really managing the team? When you're overloaded, important things are certain to be overlooked—and there's no avoiding it.

Burnout Is Exhausting

- Stress creates health problems, like those suffered by Ryan, whom you met in the introduction.

- A daily grind so taxing and toxic can defeat a high-potential employee like Amanda.

- Business problems; just ask Amanda's senior leadership how they'll cover her departure and still keep their promises to the board of directors.

- Burnout is just plain exhausting!

Turnover Is Expensive

The real cost of losing a high-value employee is far higher than most people think. Replacing somebody in a corporate environment costs between 90 and 200 percent of that employee's annual salary, according to the Society of Human Resource Management (SHRM). That cost factors in recruiting costs, training costs, and error rates in the first six months as they're learning the role and in downtime when nobody is in the job. When you realize how expensive it is to backfill a position, you have to wonder why a lot of managers or executives are not investing in saving those individuals.

If you want to decrease turnover of great talent and its associated costs, the best way to start is by taking responsibility to eliminate the Exhausted Hero predicament from your workforce.

YOUR RESPONSIBILITY

Two different circumstances, either singly or in combination, create an Exhausted Hero situation. First—in the case of Amanda and so many others like her—the company inadvertently *designed* Amanda's role to be an Exhausted Hero role. Second, Amanda never really stepped into her role as a Strategic Manager.

If you're a manager like Amanda, struggling with balance and looking to avoid burnout, it's *your* responsibility to avoid becoming an Exhausted Hero. Likewise, if you're in senior leadership (or you supervise a manager), it's *your* responsibility to help your manager(s) avoid becoming an Exhausted Hero. Yep—it's the responsibilities of both the manager *and* senior leadership to prevent the Exhausted Hero.

I wrote this book to help you understand—and master—this responsibility. The chapters ahead provide you with a simple set of tips and tools to follow, and the traps to avoid.

As a leadership development coach, I've spoken to thousands of managers and executives about how to prevent burnout. I've worked across a dozen industries—from energy to retail, from food and beverage to technology—and can tell you that no matter the field, managers and those who supervise them are struggling.

MY GOAL: RESCUE EXHAUSTED HEROES AND THE COMPANIES THAT RELY ON THEM

Amanda's experience is a true story and is one I've seen played out countless times. I put it at the top of chapter 1 because it's so illustrative of life for thousands—if not millions—of us in corporate America today. In that story, I'm not the CEO or the COO who is freaking out that Amanda quit. And I'm not Amanda.

I was the person who was in the office next door to the CHRO. As the director of talent, I regularly saw the nervous hubbub of an emergency executive meeting when yet another high-potential team member put in their two weeks' notice.

Early in my HR career, I was focused on decreasing employee turnover by facilitating workshops, implementing annual succession-planning processes, and conducting company-wide employee engagement surveys. These programs gave us the information needed to identify the issues, but they didn't provide the solutions to fix the issues. Solving the problems required individualized approaches to address the challenges of the Exhausted Heroes. With no individualized solutions, turnover continued.

Later in my HR career, I learned that individualizing retention efforts is essential in reducing turnover. We implemented leadership development programs that combined instructor-led workshops with dedicated mentors and executive coaches to individualize the learnings. We implemented executive coaching initiatives, assisting emerging leaders in avoiding becoming Exhausted Heroes. And we taught executives additional coaching skills so they could manage high-turnover-risk leaders on a day-to-day basis.

Now, my job as an executive leadership coach and consultant is to help Exhausted Heroes and the companies who rely on them. I know the differences between the story that upper management tells and the story that the disenchanted high-potential employee tells, and in a sense I'm the interpreter who helps each side understand the other better. Through integrated high-potential leadership development programs, executive coaching, and several other programs, I can help companies rescue their Exhausted Heroes and build a plan to retain and grow high-potential individuals more effectively.

MY STORY

I started out at Target Corporation in Minneapolis right out of college, working at corporate headquarters. As an entry-level business analyst, I managed the $250 million inventory for skin care for all of Target's eight-hundred-plus stores at the time. If there was a skin-care product on the shelf, I put it there.

I had a phenomenal manager, who really wanted to take care of his team, helping us to become successful and grow. So it wasn't long before I became a manager and then a buyer in charge of buying soda. In negotiating with Coke, Pepsi, Dr. Pepper, and a lot of specialty sodas, I came to really enjoy the people side of the business.

Since then I've always led teams, managing and developing others, and I have focused on elevating talent management and talent development within organizations.

I started my talent development career while still at Target, creating a training program for all new buyers. Experience in training led me to recruiting, which I did for a few years until—honestly— I grew tired of the cold climate in Minnesota. We moved back to Colorado, where I'm originally from, and I worked for Sports Authority, building the talent side of their business from the ground up. They had never had corporate-headquarters-based training, and their field organization was in need of a training reboot, so I was thrilled to lead the charge. We likewise had success in building an engagement program for leaders across the organization and then in working one-on-one, coaching executives.

At Red Robin, I built the high-potential program for both corporate and field-based emerging leaders. Then at DCP Midstream, a natural gas processor here in Colorado and a *Fortune* 500 company, I worked one-on-one with recent MBA graduates we hired every year. I also led the team that built a leadership development program, rebuilt the performance management annual review process, and managed all the talent acquisition needs.

From there I founded Game Plan Leader, where we conduct executive coaching, help build leadership programs, and facilitate workshops on rescuing the corporate Exhausted Hero. Over the years, I've become certified in a number of coaching and training programs through Gallup, the Leadership Circle, and many more.

Today, we work with some of the biggest companies and best and brightest individuals, helping them make the jump to Strategic Manager.

Publishing a book was never on my personal bucket list, but as I coached, I discovered the model of the Exhausted Hero and how much it helped managers and executives to better understand talent development. The more this idea connected with people, the more I realized this was a model that needed to be shared.

For me, I'm writing this because I have coached too many Exhausted Heroes. While there are plenty of books out there that provide a definition of management and others that define leadership, those aren't and can't be treated as mutually exclusive roles. We've got to learn to do both in a balanced way if our team members and we ourselves are going to develop our full potential, without succumbing to the Exhausted Hero trap.

With that in mind, let's circle back to the key question here: How could a manager like Amanda—and like those of her senior leadership—have done things differently to avoid turning this valuable asset into an Exhausted Hero?

CHAPTER 2

THE EXHAUSTED HERO MODEL

B ack in the day of Henry Ford and the Model T, there were many exhausted workers, but there weren't many Exhausted Heroes. The individual contributors worked hard and had little machinery to lift heavy engines or move large objects. These individual contributors were exhausted. But the role of the Exhausted Hero didn't exist, because everyone had very distinct responsibilities. The individual contributor turned the wrench, the manager supervised, and the leader created the blueprint for success.

The roles and responsibilities of the early 1900s were clear, with very defined behaviors to ensure the manufacturing line operated effectively. If there were defined behaviors in the early 1900s, I think they would have been described this way:

Individual-Contributor-Focused Behaviors

- **Drives results**: Individual contributors deliver tasks to complete a project or process. They are responsible for completing these tasks or groups of tasks in a timely and effective process.

- **Has technical/functional expertise**: Individual contributors gain proficiency and sometimes mastery of their role through technical capabilities or mastering a procedure.

- **Learns and teaches others**: Coupled with technical/functional expertise, it is important for an individual contributor to be a learner and, as they achieve expertise, a teacher of others.

Manager-Focused Behaviors

- **Manages team**: Through recognition, feedback, advice, and managing accountabilities, the manager ensures their team of individual contributors is on track to achieve the team goals.

- **Manages resources**: Through managing budget, head count, assignments, timelines, and cross-functional support, managers ensure their team of individual contributors has the resources needed to achieve the team goals.

- **Manages projects**: Managers step above the tasks and oversee the group of tasks or projects. By managing the projects to drive accountability, managers ensure the team is set up for success.

Leader-Focused Behaviors

- **Creates a vision**: A leader needs to be the guide; they must establish the purpose, build the goals, and create a vision for the future. An effective leader creates clarity, inspiration, and success with this vision.

- **Influences change**: It is important that leaders keep the business changing, evolving, and elevating. An influential leader can lead an organization down a path to the vision. Influencing could be inspiring, persuading, or gaining partnership to enable the capabilities for success.

- **Coaches others**: A manager often leads from the back: "Go do this. Why didn't you do this?" A coach leads from the front: "Come this way. How can I help? What do you need?" A coach develops their team with new skills and provides opportunities through stretch assignments.

I believe these three roles and nine behaviors are still relevant to today's workforce, but we're beginning to see these roles start to overlap and integrate, creating what I call the new seven levels of work.

In today's business world, there are efficiencies and cost savings associated with blending the three roles of the Henry Ford era. At times, we need a manager to step in and turn a wrench like an individual contributor. It could be deemed more efficient for the leader to also manage the team and run shifts effectively.

Reviewing how these roles integrate and the expected behaviors of these new roles is the key to rescuing Exhausted Heroes like Amanda.

THE EXHAUSTED HERO MODEL

To illustrate the seven new levels of work and how the three traditional roles of the individual contributor, manager, and leader have now overlapped and integrated, I've created the Exhausted Hero Model, figure 2.1. The traditional circles of influence around the individual contributor, manager, and leader remain. But the model now overlays seven new roles that exist in corporate America today. These roles are numbered in order of potential career path as we start as a Taskmaster (1) and potentially follow the entire numbered route to Visionary (7).

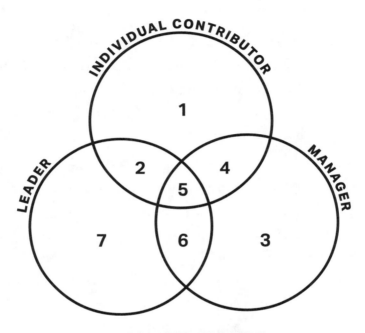

THE EXHAUSTED HERO MODEL

1. Taskmaster
2. Rockstar
3. Clipboard Manager
4. Working Manager
5. Exhausted Hero
6. Strategic Manager
7. Visionary

Figure 2.1: In many models of integration, the center represents the optimal result. In this Exhausted Hero Model, the center point, or Exhausted Hero (5), is the least optimal role.

Below are the descriptions of the seven new roles associated with the Exhausted Hero Model. These descriptions also provide a view of the associated behaviors of these new roles based on the integration of the traditional individual contributor, manager, and leader roles.

1. **Taskmaster**. The Taskmaster is an individual contributor hired to get stuff done. Their scope is relatively small, they're focused mostly on short-term task lists, and there is often a lot of repetition in their work.

   - **Associated behaviors**: Drives results, serves as technical/ functional expert, learns/teaches others

2. **Rockstar**. The Rockstar is the integration of individual-contributor and leader roles. The Rockstar continues to get stuff done but also starts working on larger projects, teaching others, and identifying and implementing more efficient and effective processes. In some organizations, this is a promotion. In others, it isn't. No matter how it is recognized, it's not rewarded with being given a team … yet. But the Rockstar's leadership and focus on the future is beginning to show.

   - **Associated behaviors**: Drives results, serves as technical/ functional expert, learns/teaches others, creates a vision, influences change, coaches others

3. **Clipboard Manager**: The Clipboard Manager has gained a team, more resources, and a broader scope. This person is paid to keep focused on today, the short term. Their focus is on managing the spinning plates. They're not tasked with adding more plates but with keeping those already spinning in motion. Clipboard Managers also drop all individual-contributor responsibilities through delegation.

   - **Associated behaviors**: Manages team, manages resources, manages projects

4. **Working Manager**: The Working Manager is the integration between individual contributor and manager. The Working Manager manages a team but also gains or retains additional individual-contributor duties. Sometimes a Working Manager is a former Clipboard Manager who has gained the efficiencies and effectiveness of managing their team, so they can now take on additional individual-contributor responsibilities. Other Working Managers may manage a small team while having the ability to maintain individual-contributor roles in meeting the needs of the business.

    - **Associated behaviors**: Drives results, serves as technical/ functional expert, learns/teaches others, manages team, manages resources, manages projects

5. **Exhausted Hero**: This role includes maintaining responsibility for individual contributors' work and managing the team, while adding the requirement of looking forward by building a vision, leading change, and influencing the future of the department or team. In other words, it combines the roles of the individual contributor, manager, and leader. This role is overwhelming, and that often shows in both results and team health.

    - **Associated behaviors**: Drives results, serves as technical/ functional expert, learns/teaches others, manages team, manages resources, manages projects, creates a vision, influences change, coaches others

6. **Strategic Manager**: These leaders represent the integration between manager and leader roles. They focus on managing their teams and planning for the future, while delegating all individual-contributor work. This allows the Strategic Manager to lead by effectively setting the vision, influencing the future, and

coaching the team to deliver results.

- **Associated behaviors**: Manages team, manages resources, manages projects, creates a vision, influences change, coaches others

7. **Visionary**: This leader is 100 percent focused on the future and delegates the day-to-day management of the vision to managers and their teams to drive. They also lead change, influence others, and coach their management team to make the vision come to life.

- **Associated behaviors**: Creates a vision, influences change, coaches others

Of all these roles, the Exhausted Hero is the least sustainable and the most at risk, which is why we want to avoid it as much as possible. The Exhausted Hero Model (figure 2.1) shows the integration point of all three circles at the Exhausted Hero role and therefore the nine associated behaviors consisting of all three circles. Oftentimes with Venn diagrams, this integration point is the optimal situation. For the Exhausted Hero, it is the least optimal and most overwhelming position.

In the Exhausted Hero Model, levels four, five, and six comprise the "Elevation Zone," where a Working Manager has the opportunity to make the leap to become a Strategic Manager.

THE ELEVATION ZONE

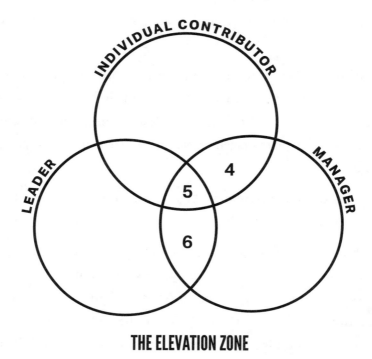

THE ELEVATION ZONE

4. Working Manager   5. Exhausted Hero   6. Strategic Manager

Figure 2.2: The Elevation Zone includes the Working Manager, Exhausted Hero, and Strategic Manager roles. This zone of career progression is a major focus of leadership development.

STUDYING THE BEHAVIORS OF THE ELEVATION ZONE

It is no surprise that there is a lot of confusion for middle management as they navigate their careers through the Elevation Zone. The focused behaviors overlap and become overwhelming to demonstrate.

A Working Manager is responsible for all of the combined manager and individual-contributor behaviors. Oftentimes, a

Working Manager may lean more on their individual-contributor behaviors than their manager behaviors.

When a Working Manager steps into an Exhausted Hero role, they are asked to display the behaviors of all three roles—individual contributor, manager, and leader. At this point, the Exhausted Hero is gaining more and more expectations and behaviors.

In comparison, a Strategic Manager is only expected to perform the behaviors of a manager and a leader. The expectations of performing individual-contributor behaviors are placed on their team. Moving from Working Manager or Exhausted Hero to Strategic Manager represents the very important process of beginning to delegate behaviors to others.

I know what you are thinking: Is it fair that the Strategic Manager isn't expected to perform individual-contributor behaviors? There is so much work to do, and everyone needs to pitch in. My answer is simple: If they focus on individual-contributor behaviors, who is focused on the important leader behaviors? Exhausted Heroes get themselves buried in tasks, and the leader behaviors become "in my spare time" behaviors. This is what creates the reactive, fire-drill, exhaustive world for the Exhausted Hero and their team.

This is a big shift in actually eliminating behaviors from their job description. By eliminating the individual-contributor behaviors, these Strategic Managers can focus solely on the leader and manager behaviors.

> **Exhausted Heroes get themselves buried in tasks, and the leader behaviors become "in my spare time" behaviors. This is what creates the reactive, fire-drill, exhaustive world for the Exhausted Hero and their team.**

This allows Strategic Managers to actually be strategic.

In a perfect world, companies would design their organizations and train their Working Managers to make the leap from Working Manager to Strategic Manager without ever stepping into the Exhausted Hero role. They would do this by maintaining their manager behaviors, dropping their individual-contributor behaviors, and adding their leader behaviors, all at the same time. This is a complicated challenge but one that is very possible.

THE PATH BEYOND THE EXHAUSTED HERO

A friend and former colleague of mine, Melissa, was a typical Corporate Exhausted Hero. Melissa achieved a long career with a large energy company that included several promotions and rewards. But as Melissa kept getting promoted, she became more and more exhausted.

Melissa started her career as an HR specialist. Immediately, she was recognized for having the ability to get things done. As a strong Taskmaster, she focused on her responsibilities day by day, received task-based assignments, and completed her work often ahead of schedule. She was quickly promoted to senior HR specialist.

As senior HR specialist, Melissa maintained her responsibilities and continued to complete her tasks ahead of schedule. Like a typical Rockstar, Melissa began to train others, get involved in larger projects, and build processes that drove efficiencies in HR. And she continued to complete her tasks, most of the time ahead of schedule.

Soon, Melissa was promoted to HR manager. She assumed the management of five HR specialists. She also gained accountability for new projects and the budget. But as a Working Manager, she continued to complete her tasks, now most of them behind schedule.

The job didn't seem different in deliverables to Melissa; the job just felt like … more!

The HR team started to fall behind, and new requests for projects were overwhelming Melissa. Melissa's boss provided feedback to Melissa that she was too reactionary and she needed to focus on being more strategic.

Now Melissa was working day and night to try to be strategic while managing her team and while completing most of her tasks, no longer on time. She was officially an Exhausted Hero.

Exhausted Heroes like Melissa fall into the same common trap—the job continues to grow, not change. Melissa's level of responsibilities grew, and so did the behaviors that were expected of her.

For the first time in Melissa's career, it was time for her to discontinue behaviors. To be an effective Strategic Manager, Melissa needed to fully step into the leader-focused behaviors of creating a vision, influencing change, and coaching others while stepping away from the individual-contributor-focused behaviors of driving results, technical expertise, and training others.

Through focused work and intentional changes within Melissa's day-to-day behaviors, Melissa has successfully elevated to the Strategic Manager role. Her team is engaged, her internal clients are thankful for a strong partner, and Melissa is energized by her job.

The Exhausted Hero Model provided Melissa with the stepping-stones to elevate to a Strategic Manager. The seven levels of work and the behaviors associated with each role provided her the map to successfully change the direction of her career.

CHAPTER 3

IT STARTS WITH TALKING ABOUT EXHAUSTION

Dennis, a senior executive at a manufacturing company, was a recent coaching client who wanted to advance himself from Strategic Manager to Visionary Leader. As he was a leader of a four-hundred-person plant, it was critical that he drive productivity by focusing on building the vision of the future, leading continuous change, and coaching. In one coaching session, it became clear that he had an Exhausted Hero challenge—but it wasn't him!

Dennis came to one of our many hour-long coaching sessions frustrated. As he was attempting to empower his managers to manage the details of the day-to-day business, one of his senior managers was not performing. Cathy had been with the plant for several years and at one point was considered high potential. But lately, Cathy always seemed to be frustrated, building adversaries and not partners in the plant. It was difficult to give her feedback because she used to be a Rockstar. Dennis didn't want to frustrate her any more than he needed to, but on this day, he was concerned that her team's performance was slipping.

"I don't want to fire her, but I don't know what else to do to help her!"

Then I asked him the question so many leaders hate to hear—but need to: "Have you asked *her* what's going on?"

Two weeks later, I met with Dennis again. He greeted me with more excitement and urgency than he had in previous sessions. He told me Cathy had come into a one-on-one meeting with him clearly fired up and upset. When he stopped the meeting and asked Cathy what was going on, she completely broke down and cried. He said that vulnerability was very uncharacteristic of Cathy.

She said that all she wanted to do was support the plant, but she couldn't focus. Just as she was getting a handle on the new QA process, Dennis had asked her to take over the packaging department. And then, the packaging supervisor quit, so she started covering for that open role too. In addition, the production manager asked her to help with a machine because she was known as the machine expert in her previous role. And she said she was behind on the reporting Dennis had asked for about quality standards.

Dennis told me that Cathy sounded like an Exhausted Hero. So he asked her an important question: "How is this affecting you?" He reported that Cathy confided that she was having trouble sleeping, she was barely eating, she was working twelve-hour days, and she just couldn't get ahead of it. She said she felt like a bad manager, a bad mom, and a grumpy person. Dennis told her they would figure it out together.

"I know she is an Exhausted Hero! What do I do now?" Dennis asked eagerly.

He and I spent the next hour discussing how to help Cathy find balance between time, resources, and quality of work. Dennis created a plan to provide Cathy with additional temporary resources while also implementing a plan to teach Cathy to delegate effectively. He also took responsibility for some strategic needs of both the QA and packaging departments that would allow Cathy to focus on execution and managing her team.

With this plan, Dennis was able to rescue Cathy from being an Exhausted Hero and enabled her to function in a Working Manager role. Cathy regained her balance, became more positively engaged with the team, and remained a key leader at the plant.

Now that Cathy could delegate, she and Dennis actively developed the new leader behaviors to ascend to Strategic Manager: creating a vision, influencing change, and coaching. Before they knew it, she was a Strategic Manager, and her career was no longer stuck.

EXHAUSTION IS NOT OK

Exhaustion needs to be addressed as soon as it's recognized, because it is *not* OK. Too many of us watch others become exhausted or are regularly exhausted ourselves. We need to take action to stop it.

It took hearing Cathy speak honestly about her exhaustion, frustration, and stress to wake Dennis up to say, "Wow, I need to step in and rescue this Exhausted Hero now, before it's too late."

> **Exhaustion needs to be addressed as soon as it's recognized, because it is *not* OK.**

The story of Dennis and his direct report Cathy is very much about the Strategic Manager recognizing the Exhausted Hero and stepping in to help. Strategic

Managers need to be able to recognize exhaustion in those around them and to take action to help their stressed-out team members. Too often leaders see signs of exhaustion and become cheerleaders: "Oh, you can do it!" Instead, they need to be willing to dig in, as Dennis did, and honestly analyze the problem and its source.

Sometimes, the Exhausted Hero may need to bring the exhaustion challenges to the discussion with the manager. Acknowledging your exhaustion to your boss can be an intimidating thing. The sit-down between the supervisor and the Exhausted Hero is an essential meeting to hash out the Exhausted Hero's issues and to work together to avoid the exhaustion traps. Not surprisingly, many shy away from asking for that kind of meeting, even though this is the first step to recovery.

Think for just a second about Amanda's situation from chapter 1. Before she quit, she had been asking for help. One week, she'd requested more head count from her boss, and in another week, she requested more time. Let's take note now that she did what most of us do—she asked for help *piecemeal*. She did it in a five-minute conversation here or there. The requests were at the ends of meetings or at the tail ends of project updates. Because she took that approach, it's likely her executive didn't piece together her bread crumbs or clues to see the challenges and exhaustion she was experiencing.

When an Exhausted Hero admits to their boss that they're burned out, it has to be seen as a stopping point. It is a moment in time that requires us to step back and focus. It deserves to be the topic of its own sit-down conversation. It can't be the last three minutes of a meeting or the last three minutes of a one-on-one. It requires you to say unequivocally, "I'm excited about the results we have. I'm excited about the direction we're going. But I'm really struggling, and I need your help balancing it all to avoid exhaustion." All it takes is being open and asking for what is needed. When an Exhausted Hero leans into their expertise, many bosses, like Dennis, are glad to step in and help. They want their team to succeed, and they don't want to lose valuable talent. But if they're not aware of the issues, they can't help.

In this chapter, we'll explore how Exhausted Heroes and senior leadership can work together to end exhaustion.

THE CONVERSATION BETWEEN THE EXHAUSTED HERO AND THEIR BOSS

I spend a *ton* of time in executive coaching sessions helping people practice having these difficult conversations with their bosses. Yes, it's intimidating to have to say, "I need help to manage the role you think I'm doing. I'm not doing well. I'm struggling. I'm exhausted." Those are not easy things to say out loud, particularly to our managers, but sometimes they need to be said. When a boss hears what you're saying and is made aware of your feelings, they usually open up and try to help solve the problem.

This feels risky, and I won't deny that the risk is real. But would you rather fail while struggling, or fail by asking for support? Bosses don't want to see their direct reports struggle, and they certainly don't want to see the projects struggle either. So, when asked to help, more often than not, they'll step in and step up.

But there are some times when … they don't. The boss might not have the big-picture awareness to understand the degree to which burnout can be so toxic for a person, a team, a culture, and a company. Plus, they might be too burned out themselves to recognize exhaustion as a problem.

I've coached a few individuals who've asked for that conversation and whose bosses effectively dismissed them with, "Just dig in and make it happen." Nobody wants to work for a boss who isn't going to support them, and usually within six months, they end up leaving, just like Amanda did.

Others have a boss like Dennis who understood the problem and helped save Cathy from exhaustion.

There's a theory that the increase in employee job-hopping has been trending because the recruiting market is so strong, and a recruiter can steal people away with just a little bit more money. I have a counter theory: I think more people are leaving their jobs because they're not getting the support they need. Rather than initiating a hard conversation, it's easier to just walk out the door—with a little increase in salary as the cherry on top. And the job-hopping continues as individuals find themselves in the Exhausted Hero trap again at the new company. The grass is not always greener!

> **I think more people are leaving their jobs because they're not getting the support they need. Rather than initiating a hard conversation, it's easier to just walk out the door—with a little increase in salary as the cherry on top.**

I know what some executives are thinking as they read this: "Are they really exhausted?" Exactly! There is a difference between being tired and being exhausted. It is comparable to what athletes experience. A long-distance runner may get tired midrace, so they walk through the water station to catch their breath—a short rest that gives them a new burst of energy to overcome being tired and keep running. Then there is the long-distance runner who leans to the side and struggles to lift one foot in front of the other. They are chronically exhausted, and it will take a major intervention for the individual to recover.

At work, it is important to ask the right questions to understand the difference between tired and exhausted. Don't just assume your direct report can figure it out on their own. If they are truly exhausted to the point that it's affecting their health and well-being, they need your help and support to overcome it.

Companies experience team-member turnover when their employees are looking for more support, more balance, and more resources to aid them in doing their jobs. If companies focused on rescuing Exhausted Heroes, they could save countless dollars in having to replace them.

> **If companies focused on rescuing Exhausted Heroes, they could save countless dollars in having to replace them.**

HOW SENIOR LEADERSHIP SUPPORTS STRATEGIC MANAGERS

Amanda might have been saved if she'd had a sit-down conversation to say, "I'm struggling. I'm exhausted. I need help delegating, or I need an executive coach to help me figure this out."

She might *not* have walked out the door if the executives had spotted the symptoms of her growing exhaustion and said, "Hold on a second. We can see that you're working a ton. I appreciate it greatly, but I also notice you're more and more stressed every day. You're not performing at your best in meetings and elsewhere. Let's pause and figure out what's going on. How can I help you?"

Unfortunately, she caught them by surprise. Her CEO and the COO didn't see the signs of exhaustion, so they didn't reach out to support her. They were almost fostering the exhaustion by giving her more work and fewer resources, and keeping her timelines.

As a senior leader, it starts with noticing exhaustion. It's important to take the pulse of your team on a regular basis. Ask yourself:

- Who is overworking?

- Who is spending more time at the office than others?

- Who is starting to struggle with thinking a process all the way through, getting stuck, and stressing out?

Senior leaders can also take the pulse on exhaustion by talking to the team, discussing project updates, observing behaviors, and understanding how direct reports spend their time. Leaders can help save an Exhausted Hero if there is awareness to spot them.

When an Exhausted Hero is identified, senior leaders can ask for help too. They can gain assistance in coaching and developing them into Strategic Managers. Hiring an executive coach can provide the Exhausted Hero with a partner to help break the habits that lead to exhaustion and build the skills needed to overcome. Senior leaders can also prioritize and invest in leadership development programs that can help proactively develop leaders to get to the Strategic Manager role faster.

AFTER THE CONVERSATION: WHERE TO START

Once Dennis realized that Cathy was exhausted, he quickly evaluated how best to offer her immediate help. Eventually, the boss should coach the Exhausted Hero on the six behaviors of the Strategic Manager, but first the supervisor should help put out the immediate fire that is creating the exhaustion. When dealing with someone who's on the brink of burnout, the boss must provide support by assisting them to evaluate three components of their current workload—

time, resources, and quality—and making adjustments where they're needed. If senior leadership pushes back, the boss must be willing to support their direct report and make a convincing case to senior leadership for the new timing, resource, or quality adjustment on their team member's behalf.

1. Time

Does the Exhausted Hero need more time? Is the pressure of the deadline exceeding the abilities of this individual to lead effectively? If so, does the deadline need to change? These are the questions a boss must ask their direct report. It may require moving the deadline of a project or pushing back the deadlines of lower-priority projects to allow the most critical deadline to be met. From the Exhausted Hero's perspective, everything is a priority and is urgent, and they don't have the perspective to evaluate the reality of the situation. That's when the boss must step up to provide the Exhausted Hero with prioritization of projects and act to adjust deadlines to give them the time they need.

2. Resources

Does the Exhausted Hero have the resources they need to complete their job? Is the Hero utilizing the resources they have as well as possible to do the job effectively? Providing more resources could mean hiring more people for the Exhausted Hero to manage or allocating them loaner people for a while. It typically starts with a conversation in which the boss asks the direct report, "Can we talk about what everybody on your team is working on?"

In Cathy's case, Dennis recognized that Cathy was trying to do too much herself and needed help delegating work to her team. After implementing these new tactics, Cathy was able to work with her team and achieve their goals.

Other times, it may be that execution is the number one priority, so Exhausted Heroes need to be geared more toward execution than toward strategic efforts. When that's the case, don't ask them for a strategic view. Let them focus on execution, and someone else can be strategic. In Dennis's case, he realized Cathy needed to temporarily be a Working Manager, so he took on the strategic projects needed for packaging and QA to allow Cathy to focus on the day-to-day needs of the departments.

3. Quality

The third essential form of support surrounds the quality expectations of the project, which should be in line with the ability of the team in place to achieve them. This means that if the deadline suddenly gets tight and the team is short on resources, but senior leaders want the project to be the highest level of quality that it can be, that combination puts a tremendous amount of stress on that small group of people who don't have the time or the resources to achieve the desired quality.

A good way to support the Exhausted Hero's quality responsibility would be to find an opportunity where the quality could reasonably decrease to 70 percent from 100 percent. This could include asking for a proposal to be limited to three pages rather than ten pages. This could include resetting the expectation that the proposed action needs to be based on their gut, not on hours of data analysis. This could include limiting customer research to three customers, not the ten originally requested. This new target would ensure that the project can still get the desired final result and can be attained without exhausting the team. And this can be done by reprioritizing the quality of *all* of the projects on this person's list, not just the one creating the most stress.

THE RESPONSIBILITY WE SHARE FOR TOMORROW

Let me make sure there is *no* confusion: building Strategic Managers and eliminating Exhausted Heroes is the responsibility of both the individual and the senior leaders of the organization. In the workplace, it's common for everybody to look around for somebody else to meet any given challenge. Stop pointing fingers, and start working together to solve the problem!

Too often, executives look at the high-potential employees or those people stuck in an Exhausted Hero role and effectively shrug it off, saying, "Well, they've got to figure it out." If that's the case, then the executives aren't taking responsibility for the culture of the team.

> Let me make sure there is *no* confusion: building Strategic Managers and eliminating Exhausted Heroes is the responsibility of both the individual and the senior leaders of the organization.

Go online and read the Glassdoor reviews page of any company out there. If you find comments from tenured employees saying things like, "These young people need to suck it up; this is business, not a playground," that's a sign the company culture and senior leadership are out of touch with their own responsibility.

At the same time, because Exhausted Heroes are so demoralized and drained, they're more likely to look for an external cause than they are to look inward. They'll wonder, "Why am I not getting help?

Why am I stuck here? Why does my boss not understand this?" They likewise are searching for somebody else to take responsibility for their exhaustion.

Both sides are failing to take appropriate responsibility. Instead of playing the blame game, look at this situation as an opportunity for better professional development, improved employee retention, and elevation of the company's culture. When it comes to an individual's development, executives and Exhausted Heroes must sit down together and say, "What is our intention? Where are we going? What are we trying to do? How are we trying to get there?"

It needs to be a mutual responsibility, because it's tough to do without both parties actively participating. The executive who says, "Hey, middle manager, figure it out," is now putting the onus on somebody who might not have the resources to handle it and who may respond by quitting. If you are the middle manager who's saying, "I need the boss to figure it out," you may get fed up with waiting and leave. Those are two ways to quickly turn future leaders with high potential in your organization into *former* employees. Instead, sit down together, show your engagement, and execute a Game Plan together.

This approach of mutual responsibility creates higher retention within these leaders. These new Strategic Managers will lead their teams in a way that will continue to grow profits for the organization. These leaders will achieve it all without doing it all.

THE IDEAL SOLUTION: A CLOSING STORY

Dennis and Cathy created a partnership. Through Dennis's ability to recognize signs of exhaustion, he was able to create a better path forward to success. Cathy is now an engaged Strategic Manager. She partners with Dennis to prioritize work, solve important problems, and align her team's projects.

Even more importantly, Dennis has created a culture focused on great results and not a culture of exhaustion. He is not sacrificing his team to create the results needed; he assists his team in finding the right balance through prioritizing their time, resources, and the quality of the work required.

By having the tough conversation, Dennis and Cathy have created a proactive culture, not a reactive, exhausting culture. Dennis and Cathy can better predict and plan the future instead of constantly being focused on digging out.

It all starts with a conversation between a supervisor and a direct report about exhaustion. Do you need to start the conversation?

CHAPTER 4

THE DESTINATION IS STRATEGIC MANAGER

Recently, an Exhausted Hero asked me if success in a Strategic Manager role is actually even achievable. Let's start by describing what a successful Strategic Manager looks like.

A Strategic Manager is somebody who has the complete buy-in of their team. They always look calm, cool, and collected, because they seem to know what's coming and how to handle it. When a fire erupts, they immediately turn into the fire chief, rather than a firefighter. They organize the team's command center (literal or metaphorical) to be able to respond before fires even start.

Day to day, Strategic Managers spend a lot of time connecting with their teams, which builds a level of trust and collaboration that just doesn't exist with teams led by an Exhausted Hero. Strategic Managers hold one-on-one meetings with individuals on their team and check in on projects—*without* diving in and executing the tasks themselves. They don't expend much time in extra computer systems; they probably don't even pull their own reports. Instead, their days are spent primarily in meetings and communicating via email, influencing change, and making sure every team member is following the same vision.

Communication is the optimal way to mobilize teams. When strategically mobilized, a team can always achieve better results than can a solo Exhausted Hero. That's why Strategic Managers invest so much time and energy into connecting with their team through one-on-one and team meetings—to mobilize more efficiently and effectively.

> **When strategically mobilized, a team can always achieve better results than can a solo Exhausted Hero.**

When not mobilizing, Strategic Managers spend their days looking ahead to anticipate what's coming and brainstorming how to influence the potential challenges in the coming weeks and months: "This project is going to miss a deadline. How do I get that in front of the people who need to know about it now?" or "We're going to need more resources on this project. Who can make time to help us?" or "We're going to need to shift this to another system. How do we do that? Let's start thinking about that now." They don't wait until the last minute to address issues, because they've seen them coming and have already anticipated potential needs and resources.

Hopefully a proficient Strategic Manager has a boss who's either a Visionary or a Strategic Manager too. Together, they spend the majority of their time talking about the future, not the past. They may talk a little bit about the present, but it's always in reference to the future. They're thinking about the next quarter, the next year, the next five years. They start by saying, "Here's what's happening on this project. This is what needs to happen in the next six months." They explore questions like, "How does this impact the team's vision? How does it impact other things, besides just this project?"

When you have all of those elements in place—when a Strategic Manager has the resources and the required self-awareness to truly be strategic—being successful is more than achievable; it's simply the nature of the role.

DEVELOPING INTO A STRATEGIC MANAGER

Chris was burned out. His senior leader contacted me to start a coaching engagement with Chris to right his ship and rescue him from exhaustion. This senior leader knew that Chris was too valuable for the organization to lose, and he was too burned out to course-correct by himself.

After speaking with Chris for five minutes on my first day coaching him, I could tell he was an Exhausted Hero. He'd been putting out fires every day for so many years that he didn't know any other way to do his job. He had no time for leading his team, let alone for creating strategy. His boss—an executive in senior leadership—knew Chris would fight fires until his health deteriorated and his team left him. But senior leadership had hope that by developing a Leadership Game Plan, we could help Chris make the jump from Exhausted Hero to Strategic Manager.

As the main "firefighter," Chris had something I've seen in thousands of Exhausted Heroes: a set of behaviors perfect for putting out fires but detrimental to leading a team and being strategic. To begin our six-month coaching relationship, we reviewed the Exhausted Hero Model and assessed his capabilities of the nine

51

focused behaviors. We also evaluated which behaviors he relied on most and which behaviors he rarely had the capability or time to display. We realized that he was trying to use all of these behaviors— and probably not using any of them well. He was an Exhausted Hero.

What did he need to start doing to become a Strategic Manager? What did he need to stop doing? For Chris to elevate out of his role as an Exhausted Hero, dropping old habits was as important as adding new behaviors.

The first step was focused on increasing Chris's time and skills in influencing change. This behavior would be essential to his success as a Strategic Manager and was a behavior with which he lacked strong competence. Although he needed to display all six behaviors associated with the Strategic Manager, focusing on influencing change would provide the biggest lift in his ability to lead.

Chris also needed to let go of his firefighter behaviors focused on personal execution. He needed to spend less time driving results and needed to no longer be the technical expert on his team.

To effectively decrease his driving results and technical expert behaviors, we determined that we would focus on delegation. If Chris was able to effectively delegate tasks and assignments, he would be less likely to take those tasks and assignments on himself, therefore creating less emphasis on his driving results and technical expert behaviors and allowing for more emphasis on influencing change. Chris had to learn to delegate.

Chris and I built a Leadership Game Plan to focus on his development. We agreed he needed coaching, mentorship, and training to help him develop behaviors to influence change and to learn to effectively drop the old behaviors by delegating.

Influencing Change

For Chris to step out of the Exhausted Hero role, the first thing he needed to do more effectively was influence change. In the past, he'd step into the change and do it all himself. Now, in order to influence the change, he had to step out of the firefight and lead people through in his place, like a fire chief as opposed to a firefighter.

After we spent some time developing his skills in one-on-one coaching so that he'd be able to better lead change, he moved to a better place. When a fire happened, instead of jumping in and fixing it himself, he would immediately mobilize the team: "All right. This just happened. Any ideas?" That was a big shift from how he'd have handled change previously. Before, he would fly through the change and hope his people would follow. If they did, the team would always be five steps behind, and therefore they couldn't help him effectively put the fire out.

Making this adjustment gave him the ability to lead change and get ahead of future fires, as opposed to just diving in himself and not thinking past the next step.

It was awesome that he could lead change and mobilize his team, but there were outside forces, other teams, that were creating the fires that he and his team were tasked with putting out. How could he better influence those other teams and change the cycle of firefighting?

A bit of backstory: Chris worked in production, but most of the fires he was stuck putting out were started by the sales department. The sales-production dynamic is a common spot for strife in most companies. Sales often sells something slightly different than the standard product that production builds, or production struggles to meet expectations set by sales. The result in both cases is typically an ignited customer fire that needs to be put out.

An example: Chris had a sales representative who habitually came in and dropped off a problem at his desk, saying, "This just happened. You've got to fix it." In disgust that another fire had been set by this individual without regard for Chris and his team, Chris would literally try to get the salesperson out of his office as fast as possible because he was so frustrated with that individual for creating the problem. Then he would dig in and put out the fire.

We began by designing a new response for Chris: "Oh, we need to go see someone else about this. Come with me." This allowed Chris to bring the sales rep into a larger discussion. The goal was to expose this person to the fire they were unintentionally setting, rather than taking it on, on his behalf. In doing so, Chris influenced the sales rep's perspective on the fires being continuously set. This helped the salesperson see: "Wait a minute. I just did this to Chris and his whole team. I've got to stop making deals that create these problems." Chris didn't have to say anything specific; he just had to invite the salesperson into the fire to start influencing change.

Chris and I worked to build his skills around influencing. We ran through a bunch of scenarios, and he began to start influencing differently. By learning how to influence people in a friendly way by saying, "Come with me; let's go figure out what's broken," it created accountability for that person and changed their behaviors going forward.

That was a big learning moment for him, and it worked like a charm. Gradually, there were fewer and fewer fires to put out.

Delegating

Step two of his Leadership Game Plan was to learn to delegate. He needed to step out of *driving results by himself* and of being the *technical expert* for his team. He likewise needed to elevate his most senior person on the team to take on more of the workload of driving results, putting out fires, and becoming the team's technical expert.

Delegation is often a skill thought of as "all or nothing": either I do it all, or you do it all and I do nothing. But there are many other ways to delegate. In our coaching sessions, Chris and I reviewed his to-do list and discussed tasks that he could potentially delegate to his direct reports. In some instances, it was easy for Chris to delegate the entire task. In others, it was more challenging. We broke down the fear of delegation into three buckets: (1) trust of the delegate's skills, (2) time to complete the project, and (3) the necessity of quality.

In many cases, we were able to delegate part of the task, but not all of the task. Sometimes he would ask someone to research and report back their findings or to put together a proposed action plan. With Chris learning to delegate, it gave his direct report the opportunity to step into the fire. Chris was able to become the team's strategic leader, giving him the perspective to see the next fire coming and to proactively try to stop it before it could start.

Also, through coaching, we identified a direct report who could step up into a technical expert role. Whenever a technical question was brought to him, Chris would first ask the new technical expert's perspective or ask them to completely step into the advisory role on a project. They also assisted all new employees in getting up to speed.

After a few months, Chris arrived at a place where he wasn't putting out fires himself at all. He'd influenced so effectively that there were far fewer fires to begin with, and he'd learned to delegate when he needed to. The technical expert on the team had stepped into their new space and helped greatly on several key projects. Chris was finally able to spend the rest of his time on being the highly effective leader his team needed.

About a week after I wrapped up my coaching time with Chris,

I got separate emails from both Chris and his supervisor thanking me for the progress we were able to make in elevating Chris. A few months later, I received another thank-you from Chris, when he shared that he'd just been promoted. He was using the same Leadership Game Plan to prepare for his new role in upper management. Chris was thrilled that he was not experiencing the burnout he'd suffered from just the year before.

THE IDEAL STRATEGIC MANAGER: TWO STORIES

Throughout my career, I've been fortunate to meet a handful of individuals who truly exemplify what it is to be a Strategic Manager.

Very early on in my career, I worked with Rick Maguire, a senior vice president of inventory management at Target. Rick's rapid response to whatever fires broke out always amazed me; either he already knew how to fix the issue, or he was able to swiftly frame the problem, mobilize the team, and move them forward. Because Rick spent so much time analyzing what was going on, analyzing what the future could be, and checking in with his leaders, he was able to see clearly where others just saw smoke.

He had checkpoints in place to make sure that what he was expecting to happen was what actually was happening. He "inspected what he expected." Rick definitely had moments when he would get upset or angry when something didn't happen, but it was usually after the plan was in place and somebody dropped the ball—not because something had happened that he hadn't anticipated. As a senior vice president and a Strategic Manager, he was able to be forward thinking and help the managers underneath him maintain a clear vision of where things stood.

For our team, Rick's foresight and clear expectations resulted in a happy, engaged, and productive work environment. It was challenging work, but I still think fondly of that experience today.

Here's a second story: I worked at a large national retailer, Sports Authority, that was implementing a new supply chain computer system. In that supply chain system, there was a new forecasting tool and a new replenishment tool to dramatically enable the organization to better manage the inventory through the supply chain and create more accurate information for long-term planning.

Lynn Morris was the senior vice president overseeing the project and one of the best leaders I've ever worked for. She was truly a Strategic Manager. Lynn inherited and elevated a team of about twenty members participating in this big change. There were two expert Working Managers reporting to her. The first of them knew everything about forecasting sales and inventory flow in that organization, and then became an expert on how to use the new tool to improve those forecasts. The second Working Manager worked on the replenishment side of things, on how to manage the flow of inventory through the supply chain.

By structuring her team in this way and delegating effectively, Lynn had the ability as a Strategic Manager to step out of the details of executing. She was able to influence senior leadership and tell them what was coming, thus getting decisions from them early in implementing the new system, because she presented all ideas to them early. She was able to set and share a fleshed-out vision for the team of what they were trying to accomplish; there were clear-cut goals. She did this through monthly meetings, where the team collaborated together and reviewed, asking questions like, "How are we doing in our work to achieve these goals? Is there anything we're doing that runs counter to the goals?" She did an excellent job of influencing change. She was always thinking six to eight months ahead, identifying what problems could arise next. What were the things that the senior leadership was going to be concerned about? What decisions would impact the success of the system implementation? She considered every question far in advance.

In addition, Lynn coached her team. She did not get into the details of replenishment and forecasting but instead coached those two Working Managers to truly own their projects and help them make decisions themselves. She didn't tell them what to do all the time. She helped them to think more constructively. Lynn was able to help them become empowered leaders in their own right, by standing up for what they were doing and how they were doing it for the organization.

To this day, if Lynn Morris (now Wiggins) were to call anyone from that team and say, "Hey, I've got a job," we would move our families to go work for her, because she built trust, understanding, and excellence. If we messed up, we knew it. But our errors were never held over our heads, because she was always so focused on the future, not the past or the present.

I asked Lynn once how she became a great Strategic Manager. She said she was a strong Working Manager who just kept taking on more and more responsibilities until she became overwhelmed. She had wished executive coaching was available but was thankful she had multiple mentors who were able to provide advice. Over time, Lynn learned how to trust and delegate to others. This gave her time to focus on strategic planning. Then, she learned to coach others. She said it was slow going at first, with a lot of trial and error, but her perseverance was what made her successful. As she became a senior leader, she spent time coaching her direct reports in becoming better leaders and supported their participation in executive coaching and leadership development programs.

LET'S DEVELOP MORE STRATEGIC MANAGERS

Rick, Lynn, and Chris all elevated to become effective Strategic Managers who leveraged their manager and leader behaviors while delegating their individual-contributor behaviors to their teams. Their leadership enabled their teams to find success without exhaustion.

Chris found success by creating and executing a Leadership Game Plan. Later in this book, we will provide additional structure and tips to create an effective Leadership Game Plan. But for now, I want to emphasize that an Exhausted Hero can elevate to a Strategic Manager role.

CHAPTER 5

THE COMMON PATH TO STRATEGIC MANAGER

The path from Exhausted Hero to Strategic Manager can include a tough climb. The executives who can ascend the path will find great success and be viewed as strong leaders in their organizations. The executives who fail to get to leadership and continue to flounder in execution will struggle to keep their heads above water.

To be an effective Strategic Manager like Rick, Lynn, or Chris, the Strategic Manager should focus on the following behaviors:

- Manager-focused behaviors: manage team, manage projects, and manage resources

- Leader-focused behaviors: create vision, influence change, and coach others

For the majority of the Exhausted Heroes whom I have coached successfully to become Strategic Managers, the key to the elevation has been learning the skills of the leader-focused behaviors. The

Exhausted Hero realizes that these new leader behaviors represent their new role and that the individual-contributor-focused behaviors can no longer take up their valuable time and energy.

The manager-focused behaviors are rarely the focus of coaching engagements for Exhausted Heroes. Exhausted Heroes have often been learning and implementing manager-focused behaviors for years as a Working Manager and Exhausted Hero. Because this is rarely the focus for Exhausted Heroes, I will not be focusing on manager-focused behaviors for the remainder of the book. That doesn't mean that they aren't important; it just means I am going to focus the remainder of the book on what I believe

For the majority of the Exhausted Heroes whom I have coached successfully to become Strategic Managers, the key to the elevation has been learning the skills of the leader-focused behaviors.

most Exhausted Heroes will use. If an Exhausted Hero finds that the manager-focused behaviors are a challenge, I highly encourage investigating manager-skills workshops and identifying other resources to assist.

For the majority, the transformation from Exhausted Hero to Strategic Manager lies in gaining the skills of creating a vision, influencing change, and coaching others. And it also includes the challenge of delegating what drives results, being a technical/functional expert, and the learning/teaching behaviors associated with individual-contributor behaviors.

In this chapter, let's explore these important leader behaviors and understand the process of delegating the individual-contributor behaviors.

CREATING A VISION

In a recent survey by the Strategic Thinking Institute of five hundred managers at twenty-five companies, managers said their number one barrier to creating a clear strategy is time. Many managers pointed out that time spent thinking strategically is not one of the metrics by which their performance is measured. With time being a commodity, creating a vision is often overlooked, despite it being a key behavior needed by Strategic Managers.

Establishing a path forward for the next six months, year, or three to five years is creating a vision. This path provides clarity during decision-making, direction to a large number of team members, and alignment across teams as they all march forward to achieve their team's goals.

Brian was an executive at an oil and gas company and a former coaching client of mine. When we began our coaching engagement, Brian was soon to be promoted to a new role within the company that broadened his strategic responsibilities and expanded the size of his team.

In his new role, he had aspirations of blazing a new path and building a new strategy for success. He knew that his new team needed a clear vision and clear expectations. He spent the first month in his new role conducting research. He read industry trade magazines, took peers out to lunch to ask them their perspective about the business, and visited the employees out in the field organization to gain their view.

Brian also conducted a "start/stop/continue" exercise with his new direct reports, asking their perspective of what the team needed to start doing, stop doing, and continue doing.

With all of this research, Brian and his team developed a vision statement that clarified where the team was going, not where the team had been. It focused on key deliverables that provided guidance for decision-making at all levels of the organization.

Because of Brian's leadership, his team was energized by the clear vision, and they aligned to achieve success together.

A Strategic Manager spends time conducting research, meeting with industry leaders, brainstorming with their teams, and attending conferences. They utilize this information to form a vision statement with their team. The vision must be simple and easy to repeat. It must be solid and create clarity for decisions. And it must be shared often to ensure there is alignment across the team. The more a Strategic Manager can remind all partners and team members about the vision, the better. This will create an alignment that will enable the Strategic Manager to influence change almost effortlessly.

> **The vision must be simple and easy to repeat. It must be solid and create clarity for decisions. And it must be shared often to ensure there is alignment across the team.**

INFLUENCING CHANGE

The second behavior of the Strategic Manager model is influencing change. David Leonard and Claude Coltea of Gallup assert that 70 percent of all change initiatives fail because change agents overlook the role frontline managers play in the success of an initiative.[1] Companies delegate "change management" to a select "change man-

---

1   Claude Coltea and David Leonard, "Most Change Initiatives Fail—But They Don't Have To," *Gallup Business Journal*, May 24, 2013.

agement team" instead of asking all managers to influence change on their teams.

To effectively influence change, every manager needs to first understand where each team member is on the change curve. The change curve simplifies much of what's so messy about our natural responses to change. By understanding this curve and how to apply it to the team, influencing change can be a cinch!

Tool: The Kubler-Ross Change Curve

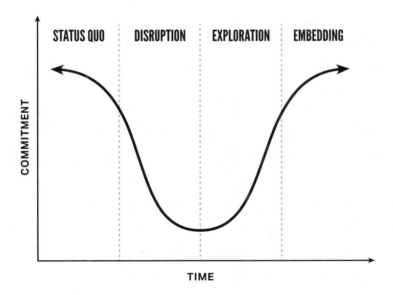

Figure 5.1: The Kubler-Ross change curve

The Kubler-Ross change curve is used in many fields, and I find it's equally helpful in strategic management. This curve is not reserved for members of the change management team; it should be used by all leaders and managers to help guide their teams effectively. The x-axis represents time, with the left end representing the beginning of a change and the right end representing the end. The y-axis represents the level of commitment to the change. The bottom end represents low commitment to the change, and the top end represents high commitment. When change arrives, we all follow a similar path to respond to and experience change.

The first stage is **status quo**. Change interrupts the status quo, and the response is, "Huh, interesting idea. I wonder what will happen with this change." Commitment is relatively high because the initial awareness of a pending change is often not that stressful. That status quo is quickly interrupted with, "We can't do this, because that's not how we do things." This is the beginning of the normal dip in the change curve.

The downward but forward-moving part of the change curve is the next stage, **disruption**. In anger and fear, many ask, "Can we really do that? That's a lot of change. How would that work?" If leaders are looking to eliminate disruption, don't! It will happen in even the best change circumstances. The change from the norm will always create some discomfort, and a barrage of questions will ensue to try to better understand the change. Clear and frequent two-way communication can make this stage short.

As the curve trends upward, we hit the **exploration** stage. That's where we're starting to put positive steps in place, come up with our ideas, put together the plan, and gain momentum in implementation. This step focuses on getting to the end of the change, not focusing on staying in the status quo. A manager in this stage helps move the team through solutions, brainstorm innovation, and design training. The commitment is rising again.

At the top of the other side of the curve is **embedding**, where the change is the new normal. Team members participate in training or gain access to new processes. Many don't see the change anymore. Instead they see it as the new status quo; it's embedded in everything that they do.

The leader who is creating the vision is probably comfortable with disruption and excited to start exploring. But what happens when the leader takes the vision of change to their direct report? The leader may be ready for exploration—as they've thought through what this change could be and have already mentally overcome any disruption—but their direct reports are likely sliding from status quo to disruption on the change curve. Shocked and fearful, they may not be ready for exploration. They may be wondering things like this:

- "Am I going to have to stop using this program that I love?"

- "Am I going to have to spend less time doing something I enjoy?"

- "Is this really going to work?"

- "How much is this going to cost?"

If someone stays in disruption mode, they often get disgruntled. That's when the gossip train at the water cooler begins. And that's where you could get some derailers—people who actively try to derail the project or change.

When it comes to influencing change, a Strategic Manager must recognize where they personally are in relation to where someone else is on the change curve. They ask themselves how they can help others catch up quickly and smoothly. Just telling someone, "Don't worry about the change; it'll be OK" doesn't work.

There are a handful of established ways to influence change and help move someone along the change curve:

- Influence with data—show reports, research, and data.

- Appeal to success—highlight the wins of making this change.

- Use logical persuasion—go through the steps of the change

with direct reports in a logical way to explain how the process will work.

- Appeal to your employees' values—align the change with what's more important to them.

- Consult—ask for other opinions and expertise. Ask others to add to the vision and therefore move along the change curve.

Beware of using the same established ways of influencing change over and over again. Take, for example, the first one I listed—influencing with data. An Exhausted Hero could easily get to a place where they are always relying on data to influence their direct reports. But maybe that's not how the team wants to be influenced; maybe they would respond more to an appeal to their values than to a presentation of data. As much as the data says there needs to be a certain change, it could still cause a lot of disruption for the team, and that's going to create issues that will not be supported by the data. Oftentimes we try to influence others the way in which we'd be most readily influenced ourselves, but we need to be more focused on influencing our teams based on the ways in which *they* need to be influenced.

COACHING YOUR TEAM

Sometimes the fastest way to solve a problem is a straight arrow, and that's a directive: tell somebody exactly what you want them to do. This can be a trap for a leader! The more time a manager spends telling their team exactly what to do, the more they're going to keep coming back to the manager with every little question, simply bringing the manager more problems to solve. Managers then return to the individual-contributor role, solving problems as opposed to thinking strategically about what's coming.

Coaching is about taking a little bit longer up front to process the perspectives of the challenge and make sure everybody is aligned with the vision. It is a deeper conversation between a manager and a direct report with questions and discussion, not a shallow discussion with only direction. The direct reports must understand their role in bringing the vision to fruition, then be trusted to execute it. Coaching is about discussing the entire project, whereas directive is discussing only the very next step. Here is a quick tool to help illustrate the skill of coaching.

Tool: The Twenty-Minute Conversation and the Coaching Curve

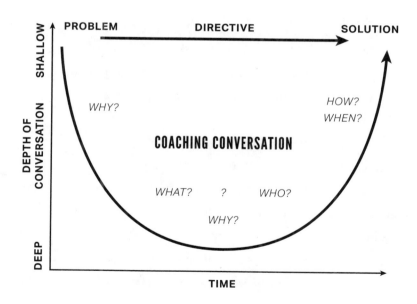

Figure 5.2: The coaching curve represents a twenty-minute conversation focused on coaching, not being directive. The conversation is deep, is full of questions, and clarifies perspectives.

This coaching-curve graphic reflects the importance of having an early conversation with a direct report about the paths ahead. Instead of giving them direction, as indicated by the directive arrow at the top of the graphic, take the longer, deeper path to ensure both the manager and direct report have a clear understanding of the challenge and solution. Take time early in the process to ask them questions and get them thinking about the problem. The following questions can help the direct report process and determine the path forward:

- What do you think is going to be the most challenging?

- What are the things that you're most concerned about?

- What are the resources you're going to need to be able to do it?

- What do you think are potential roadblocks?

Notice that the manager is not asking, "How are you going to complete the task?" The above open-ended questions are designed to get them thinking, owning, and understanding the process to achieve the vision.

Let's pretend there is a twenty-minute period between a manager and a direct report dedicated to discussing a project.

The first five minutes of the conversation should be on aligning the goals and objectives of the initiative, the *why*. It is important to ensure both parties are aligned on the desired end result.

The middle ten minutes should be spent collaboratively *exploring the problems and opportunities—the what, who, and more why.* Ask questions to get the direct report to think beyond today. So many of us, especially as Exhausted Heroes, would rather save time in the moment and skip these ten minutes because we've got too much on our minds already. But taking this time now is going to save the manager and direct report time in the long run. The key to the middle ten minutes is for the manager to ask as many questions as needed to get the direct report thinking as much as possible. Get them to see it from many different perspectives so that when they are set loose, the manager has confidence they have a full view of the challenge ahead and that they will feel empowered to drive the final result.

Spend the last five minutes of the conversation covering what the immediate next steps are, based on the discussion. This answers the questions about *how* and *when*. The manager can course-correct a little bit in coaching but, in the end, leave them feeling empowered to chase the clear objective both have set together. Then, the direct report will be on their way to get started!

Many Exhausted Heroes get addicted to the adrenaline of being directive and focusing on achieving. This is rushing those middle ten minutes and getting too directive, too quickly. The Exhausted Heroes may feel good in the short term at getting a task off the list, but their team will be back quickly to receive more direction. The Exhausted Hero will again wonder if the individual can think for themselves.

In the rush of getting started, other Exhausted Heroes rush the last five minutes of defining the next steps. It's a common but big mistake to say, "OK, now go. Good luck." The managers should fear that what they expect to be delivered may not be delivered effectively due to pure confusion. So, in those last five minutes, determine the following: Should the direct report come back with a proposal, or with research? Or is the manager looking for them to come back with a report on what they did? Defining what both parties are looking for in those last five minutes is critical. Otherwise, the team comes back with something that is not what the manager was expecting, and now the Exhausted Hero will have to jump back in as an individual contributor to fix it.

By taking more time to have a full conversation *together* as opposed to directing and instructing, the manager creates the space to make magic happen. The direct report will be more empowered. They'll be able to do more than one task at once. The manager is developing them to be more strategic because they are thinking beyond today. And ultimately, the process is creating another great leader on the team—all thanks to a simple coaching curve and a twenty-minute conversation.

By taking more time to have a full conversation *together* as opposed to directing and instructing, the manager creates the space to make magic happen.

MINIMIZING THE INDIVIDUAL-CONTRIBUTOR BEHAVIORS: DELEGATING

I was recently brought in to do a leadership workshop for a large national retailer. The VP who hired me to do the work was someone I coached years ago. When I'd coached her, we had focused on delegating, and mastering that skill was the key to elevating her from an Exhausted Hero to a Strategic Manager. Now, she was leading an organization with a culture of exhaustion, and she needed my help implementing a customized leadership development program.

During the training, I brought out my all-time favorite book, *The One Minute Manager Meets the Monkey*, by Kenneth Blanchard. This book is all about delegation. As a manager, sometimes you take on everybody else's monkeys, and all the monkeys end up on your back. Managers need to learn how to delegate effectively. By assigning the monkeys to the employees who ought to be responsible for them, the monkeys can be better managed and cared for appropriately, and the manager isn't crushed under their weight.

When I started talking about this in the workshop, the vice president immediately started giggling. I said, "What?" and she told the entire group, "This is a distinct moment in my career. When I got promoted to director and I was coaching with you, you gave me this book. It was a moment when I realized that my job had changed to more strategic leader as opposed to the doer. How you coached me through that helped me become the leader I am today. That was a defining moment in my career."

That same day, she bought her entire team that book. She realized it was important for her, and now she wanted to pass it on to others.

In her case, when she got promoted to director, she worked hard to become strategic in helping elevate the people reporting to her. Delegating strategically was a skill she realized she needed to learn early. It's one many of us must add so that we have time to do the first three skills described at the beginning of this chapter.

I've found the simplest way to explain *how* to delegate is to start with this graphic of a sliding scale in a two-headed arrow:

Tool: The Delegation Arrow

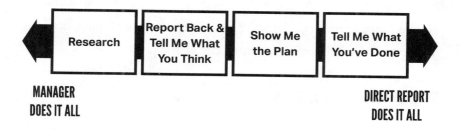

Figure 5.3: On the left end is the overcommitted manager who says, "Don't worry; I'll do it all." On the other end is the hands-off manager who says, "I don't even want to touch any of this; go do it," and just prays it gets done correctly. Neither strategy is good delegation.

The key to delegation is to think of it in four steps, indicated by the four steps in the center of the graphic—which are each their own conversation. Exhausted Heroes don't have to delegate the whole thing and forget about it, risking their reputation and the project. Managers can get the project off their plate and at the same time help in the direct report's development by having them complete one of these four steps:

1. Research.

2. Report back and tell me what you think.

3. Show me the plan.

4. Tell me what you've done.

Research

"Go research this and come back and tell me what you learned. It's not about a proposal or taking any action. Just go research and come back and tell me what you find out."

This saves the manager some time in conducting the research while also allowing the manager to make the final conclusions based on the research and build the plan to take action. It teaches the direct report how to find the information needed to make decisions. Notice that although this saves the manager time, it doesn't limit the manager's impact on the final outcome of the project.

Report Back and Tell Me What You Think

"The next step is to tell me about the research, and your conclusions and perspective on what you found." This is not the same as asking for a full-blown proposal. Managers also don't expect them to take any action but just to explain their ideas about what the action plan ought to be: "This is what I think we should do." This helps the direct report to start applying the research and start thinking strategically, but the boss is not making them go through all the steps of a formal proposal. Again notice that although this saves the manager time, it doesn't limit the manager's impact on the final outcome of the project.

Show Me the Plan

By asking them to build the action plan, the manager is asking them to think through all the steps to achieve success on the project but not asking them to initiate anything! This helps the direct report to start applying the research and start thinking strategically by putting it all together in a detailed plan. And the manager can always course-correct their plan through coaching before any action is taken. Again notice that although this saves the manager a ton of time, it doesn't limit the manager's impact on the final outcome of the project.

Tell Me What You've Done

The last step is for the direct report to go do it and then come back and tell the manager what they've done. This fourth step is the only point at which action actually happens that the manager can't easily course-correct. This is the most limiting for a manager, because if something goes wrong, they have to step in and help clean it up. That said, this is or should be the end goal of all managers: to be aligned and have direct reports whom the manager trusts to take independent action.

For each direct report, a manager should identify which bullet of delegation they are most comfortable with initiating. Then they should build an intentional plan to develop each direct report to move from the left to the right. For example, say that the manager has an employee who is definitely in the research-and-report mode. But the manager doesn't really trust him to build an action plan yet. The goal over the next few months would be to work with them to move to the next phase and learn how to build an action plan.

When this employee turns in their research report, the next project should ask them to build an action plan. If the manager doesn't delegate and they continue to stay in the research and reporting phases forever, *the manager* risks becoming an Exhausted Hero. By getting them moving more and more to the right on the delegation arrow, the Exhausted Hero will have more and more capacity to be a Strategic Manager.

Every manager should have a list or matrix of their employees, plotting their steps on their individual journeys across the delegation arrow. With such a list, a manager is never lost. They always know where their people are and how they should help them develop.

ELEVATE TO A STRATEGIC MANAGER

As I noted earlier in this chapter, the path for an Exhausted Hero to elevate to Strategic Manager includes the full adoption of the leader-focused behaviors. It is also important that the Exhausted Hero focuses on delegating the individual-contributor-focused behaviors.

The leader-focused behaviors of a Strategic Manager can't be delegated. Remember, Strategic Managers can delegate individual-contributor tasks to a direct report. But managers can't ask direct reports to take the lead in building a strategy, influencing change, or coaching themselves. That is the new role of the Strategic Manager.

The tools throughout the next chapter should provide you with tips and ideas to start implementing immediately. There is no time to waste. Your team is depending on you.

CHAPTER 6

CREATING YOUR LEADERSHIP GAME PLAN

Whether you are part of a large organization with dedicated investment in leadership development or not, you will not be rescued from being a Corporate Exhausted Hero unless you build an individualized Leadership Game Plan.

I am not talking about the old-school process of individual development plans (IDPs) that HR makes everyone fill out, which usually get stuffed in a file cabinet until annual review time. People get fired up and overly ambitious, wanting to accomplish everything at once. Those development plans can get too long and too comprehensive.

Real change takes time and consistent effort, and leaders are more likely to accomplish those goals through smaller, more concentrated efforts. Old habits die hard, and establishing new ones is challenging. That's why creating an actionable, viable Leadership Game Plan has to start with keeping them simple. How simple?

I recommend no more than two or three bulleted goals or actions that Exhausted Heroes can really concentrate on keeping alive throughout the year.

The Leadership Game Plan should include two parts: behaviors to elevate, and behaviors to minimize. Yes, I said *minimize*, if not eliminate. This is a big difference from the old HR IDPs. The Leadership Game Plan focuses on what to do more, and what to do less. The old HR IDPs were focused on adding more and more expectations.

> **The Leadership Game Plan should include two parts: behaviors to elevate, and behaviors to minimize.**

This game plan is to level expectations by adding *and* subtracting expectations.

The game plan should start by considering the behaviors to build on. List one or two of the leader behaviors that you need to elevate above where they are now. These go back to the nine behaviors tied to the model. Most Exhausted Heroes know they need to spend more time focused on creating a vision, influencing change, coaching others, managing teams, managing projects, or managing resources.

The second part of the Leadership Game Plan is to pick one behavior that you want to drop or de-escalate. Again, pick one behavior, not twenty, that you want to do less of and that is creating issues within your leadership. For most Exhausted Heroes, this means de-escalating their individual-contributor behaviors, including drive for results, serve as a technical/functional expert, or learn/teach others. This is also known as delegating more effectively.

The third part of the Game Plan is to create an actionable plan of development focused on the behaviors. These actions or activities should promote practice and utilization of these new leadership behaviors. You select two or three activities for each one of the behaviors that you want to improve or elevate. Remember, focus on only one or two targeted behaviors.

The Leadership Game Plan in Three Steps

1. Identify one to two leadership behaviors to elevate.

2. Identify one leadership behavior to drop or de-escalate.

3. Create an actionable plan to practice and use these new leadership behaviors.

To best support Exhausted Heroes in building their Leadership Game Plan, here are some ideas for activities and actions that could elevate the leader-focused behaviors or assist in developing the skill of delegating individual-contributor behaviors. Again, don't sign up to do them all. Choose one or two activities from the lists below that will successfully elevate your leadership.

CREATING A VISION SKILL DEVELOPMENT

As a Strategic Manager, focus on building a clear vision for the team to follow. How are you gathering information that will form the vision for your team? It is your role to create the vision forward that enables your team to be empowered to make that vision happen. Exhausted Heroes often create a vision in their spare time, and that doesn't work. By developing the behavior to create a vision, you will create a clear path forward for you and your team to follow. You will establish clear expectations that will enable your team to do the work instead of you. Remember, creating a vision takes time and energy.

Here are eight possible activities to help you create a better vision. Choose two or three that will work best for you.

Block Out Time for Research

I had a client who blocked out every first Friday of the month from eight to ten o'clock in the morning on their calendar and devoted it to googling what was going on in their industry. They also used the time to read the articles they'd earmarked during the course of the month about current events in their industry.

Depending on your field, your research could cover emerging technology in your industry or novel marketing efforts. What new services are your competitors offering? If you're in the oil industry, that might mean learning about how geologists are determining where to drill for oil; if you're in retail, you might look at new trends around merchandise displays. What matters most here is scheduling the time to do the research. Use it as planned time rather than leaving it for your "free time" and never really getting it done.

Attend an Industry Conference

Personally, I am a big fan of conferences, because hearing what others are doing in my industry is inspiring. It's a great way to learn about the innovation and transformation of your industry to influence your strategic perspective. I went to a conference recently around the HR space to learn how companies are applying organizational development to their organization. I learned about the new trends in performance management and talent management. Learning what other leaders in this space were doing influenced the vision that I had for my own talent philosophy. We don't have to reinvent the wheel!

Ask Your Team about Innovation

Asking your team about innovation is a way to accomplish a couple of important things. First, you're collecting ideas beyond just your own. You're getting the benefit of their industry knowledge and the research they have done. Pay attention to how they respond to your request for their ideas. Are they excited to share them, or are they hesitant to speak up? If it's the latter, you might need to consider whether you've been (consciously or not) discouraging an innovative culture. Are you promoting a work environment in which they will be part of the vision and innovation, or have they been shut out or shut down, becoming discouraged about making a contribution? If

that's the case, it's important to schedule some innovation workshops with your team. Make sure that you're asking more questions than you are making statements. Get them comfortable with sharing their ideas as opposed to just listening to yours.

I worked with the head of a recruiting organization who was struggling with his team

> **Make sure that you're asking more questions than you are making statements. Get them comfortable with sharing their ideas as opposed to just listening to yours.**

always being on their heels. He set up brainstorming sessions to get everybody to come forward and share their ideas, because he saw that he needed to shut off the part of his brain that was driving the results.

Talk with an Innovative Leader at Your Company

Seek out the people in your company who are doing well, whose teams seem to always be innovating. Ask them about how they drive innovation on their team. Talk to them about their future vision and what influences that vision. When I was a buyer at Target, I put a lot of thought into how I could drive innovation within the department for which I was responsible. I reached out to somebody whose department was doing very well, who was known for their new and creative ideas and for having a very clear strategy that his team supported. I sat down with him and some of his team and asked them about their strategy, how they had rolled it out, and what ideas or advice they could offer me on how to do something similar in my own area. I walked away with a ton of great ideas on how to involve others and really influence transformation.

Talk with an Innovative Customer

We often forget that our customers and vendors are in the same industry that we are, and they're an excellent point of reference as we think about strategy and innovation. They can be great partners for us as well. Back in my Target days, one of my favorite vendors was Jones Soda. The CEO of that company was an extremely innovative, transformational leader who had a lot of industry knowledge. For me, to sit down and just pick his brain about what was going on in the industry—what he was worried about, what he was excited about—gave me a lot of ideas about how to structure the vision for my department. And honestly? It's great customer relations too!

Visit a Different Industry

If you truly want to be innovative, get out of the comfort zone of your own expertise and your own industry. See how leaders in other businesses are addressing their challenges and solving problems. Even ask for a tour. How have they innovated?

I once coached a leader of a franchise hair salon company when

CREATING YOUR LEADERSHIP GAME PLAN

she was trying to come up with effective new ways to launch new products. I told her, "Let's think about the vision of what you're trying to do with new products. What is your mission around new products, and how do you want to drive that forward?" I asked her to do homework by actually going to different kinds of retailers outside the salon space—to malls, car dealerships, restaurants, and websites—to see how other retailers were promoting their new products. Not only did she bring back a lot of great new ideas, but she also returned with a different perspective on creating a vision around new products.

Create a North Star Mission Statement

Come up with a mission statement with your team as a North Star for everyone to follow. This way everybody's in agreement, and everybody has a say on the direction of where your team is going. Ask your team to do some research ahead of a meeting and to come up with some words that resonate for them around what they want the department to stand for. And once you've crafted a statement that's both simple and powerful, publicize it. Too often these great mission statements get stuck in a folder, and then you don't see it for months and months. Try this instead: When you have a team meeting, always put the mission statement at the top of the agenda. As you're making decisions or debating about next steps, you can refer back to the mission statement as a guide to really help you make the decisions as a team. Let it be the standard against which every action is judged.

You can refer back to the mission statement as a guide to really help you make the decisions as a team. Let it be the standard against which every action is judged.

The other big benefit of having a great mission statement is that it helps your team to make better decisions, enables them to make those decisions more quickly, and creates real empowerment for them. They're empowered to follow the mission, as opposed to having to wait for individual task direction. That frees you to be less of an individual contributor and step into the role of a strategic leader, which lessens the chance you'll become an Exhausted Hero.

Review Project Plans to Ensure They Align with the Vision for the Team

Once you've got your mission statement in hand, go back and review the active projects to make sure that they're all in alignment with the mission. If not, you might need to change the mission statement, or you may need to change the projects that are assigned. You may decide, "We don't need to do this project because it's not going to get us to where we want to go."

INFLUENCING CHANGE SKILL DEVELOPMENT

As you think about what goes into being a Strategic Manager versus an Exhausted Hero, remember that an Exhausted Hero is somebody who is driving change themselves. They are taking on tasks they shouldn't and running around putting out fires when they arise within the business. In contrast, a Strategic Manager will influence change and get ahead of those fires. It is about looking at the vision that you have set for the organization and anticipating roadblocks that may occur. It is identifying where misalignment may arise, whether from your team, peers, leaders, customers, or vendors. Where is misalignment happening, and how do you influence that alignment getting back in line before it becomes a problem?

This is a powerfully proactive mode for a Strategic Manager, as opposed to an Exhaustive Hero's typically reactive mode. By influencing change and creating a vision for others to follow, you are becoming a fire chief who is responsible for mobilizing your team, not for directing your team or leaping into the fires yourself.

> **By influencing change and creating a vision for others to follow, you are becoming a fire chief who is responsible for mobilizing your team, not for directing your team or leaping into the fires yourself.**

Once again, here are seven activities that you could incorporate into your Leadership Game Plan, this time to assist with influencing change. Choose only two to three activities that will help you.

Create an Influence Plan

Identify key partners that will have influence on the outcome of your team's projects. Create a one-page document that lists each of these partners and key areas over which they have influence. Then add a column where you can brainstorm how to best influence each individual.

I recently worked with an advertising agency that's implementing changes within their organization, including implementing a new computer system. In planning the implementation, the first task we completed was to identify the individuals and the groups that will be affected by this new system. We then identified what the big changes were, whether it be in process, in outcome, or in tasks that they need to complete. We identified what was going to be different; then we took some time to evaluate by asking those who were going to be most impacted questions about their comfort levels with these coming changes. That gave us a good indication of which groups were going to be most impacted. Knowing who'd be the most impacted let the company put together plans for communication and training, so that when the change came, it wouldn't present such a disruptive challenge. Again, this enabled leaders to be proactive, not reactive.

Hang Up the Change Curve in Your Office

As you meet with your team, realize that you are probably more accepting of the change than they are. Ask them about their discomforts and concerns. Explain the plans and ask for help filling in the strategy. Hanging the change curve in your office is a great way to remind you that you may be further along on the change curve—in the exploration and embedding phases of the change—than the people within your team are. They may have more fears and more questions; they may still be in disruptive mode because they don't truly understand what's going to happen yet. Having the change curve in your view daily reminds you to ask them, "How are things going? What makes you nervous about the change?" When you're aware of their feelings, you can provide them with the information and the guidance they need to move forward with them. I used this to help managers at Sports Authority guide their teams through a major system change, and it made managing expectations and natural anxieties much smoother.

Start/Stop/Continue

Start/stop/continue exercises are a great way to generate ideas among your team to focus on improvements and innovation. This exercise forces a leader to listen, which can be a challenge when we're in solution mode, yet empowers everybody to speak up. All it takes to do a start/stop/continue exercise is three giant Post-its or a whiteboard on which you make lists of answers from your team under the following headings: "What do we need to start doing? What do we need to stop doing? What do we need to continue doing?" Sometimes people do this toward their vision. Sometimes they do it toward how they interact with each other. But the beauty of start/stop/continue exercises is that they not only give you the chance to hear great ideas from your team, but they also encourage change. Answers to the *continue* and *start* questions provide the needed direction, while the *stop* question's answers identify barriers to success.

I had a recently promoted client who used a start/stop/continue exercise as a way to gain buy-in from her new team, to get a clear picture of what their vision was, and to get ideas about how to continue and enhance the vision in her new role. It opened up dialogue and partnership and took down many of the barriers that were there in previous conversations.

Schedule and Conduct Regular 1:1 Meetings with Employees

When we think about influencing change, a big part of it is keeping a pulse check on what's working and what's not. The best way of doing that is asking people one-on-one on a consistent, regular basis how they're experiencing change. Where we often get in trouble is when we just ask, "Hey, how're things going?" and hear something like, "Good." That's not productive. Leaders need to ask more open-ended questions to stay up to speed with what's going on and what's happening, and we do that by holding regular one-on-one meetings with our employees to gauge how they're feeling.

Many managers tell me they don't have time to schedule one-on-ones, or that they're not valuable. Others use them as a chance to ask the team member, "Did you accomplish the five things I told you to do last week? And here are five more things you need to accomplish." That's not valuable. But the pulse check—what is working, what isn't working, and what they are struggling with—is critical to a leader's ability to influence change, anticipate or mitigate roadblocks, and keep people moving forward.

Seek Additional Information

When delivering a message you don't totally understand or align with, seek additional information so that you can deliver a unified message. I coach many leaders who are nervous to bring the team together because they don't understand the change themselves, or they don't support what is going on within the organization. But at this point, it's the responsibility of the leader to step in and try to understand the issues better so they can help their team. That means they need to go to their boss and say, "I need to communicate to my team what's going on, but I don't understand it myself. I need you to walk through the benefits of this change to understand the next steps of what's going to happen." Having those conversations makes it possible for managers to return to their teams with answers and keep them in alignment with what's going forward.

Create and Implement a Leader Communication Plan

Create and implement a leader communication plan that focuses on a consistent cadence of communication with your team and client partners. As I mentioned earlier in another context, I was once involved in a computer system update that was going to be a major change within the organization. We identified a group of leaders who were going to have a big impact on whether or not it succeeded, but who tended to struggle with change. We needed the eight of them on board, so we came up with a clear communication plan that focused on a consistent cadence of meetings. We each "adopted" one of these leaders. We met with our adopted leader on a monthly basis to walk them through the change curve, get their perspective and concerns, provide them with proactive information about what was coming, and give them speaking points to give to their team around the change. That created clear and consistent communication to their teams and was a great success in winning over these reluctant change agents.

Create a "Good Communication" Folder

This is a great tool if you struggle to write as well as you'd like to, or if you'd like to improve on your communication skills. When you receive a well-written email, save it and put it in this folder. Over time, this folder will fill with emails that can serve as inspiration as you craft important communication.

This is a trick I learned years ago at Target. When I needed to craft a powerful email to my team or to my boss, I would read through the folder of emails. I would find a similar type of communication and copy the structure or borrow key words. Over time, I was able to create my own communications from scratch. But those emails helped create the templates to my success in becoming a better communicator.

COACHING SKILL DEVELOPMENT

To avoid becoming an Exhausted Hero, you need to limit being directive and learn to be a better coach. Being directive is telling people task by task what they need to do. Coaching is about stepping back, looking at the entire project together, and saying, "Here are our goals. What are our roadblocks? What do we think are going to be challenges? Whom do we need to align?" It's asking a lot of questions to get the team to see the big picture so they are empowered to go figure out how to manage and execute the plan. By coaching more than being directive, the leader has more opportunity to be in that leadership space of creating vision and influencing change, as opposed to being in the individual-contributor space.

> **Coaching is about stepping back, looking at the entire project together, and saying, "Here are our goals. What are our roadblocks? What do we think are going to be challenges? Whom do we need to align?"**

Choose two to three actions from the eight listed below that can help you elevate your game in coaching others.

Conduct Regular 1:1 Meetings

As previously mentioned, regularly scheduled one-on-one meetings are a great way to start to ask more questions and make fewer statements. Focus on helping your direct reports think through the process of their decisions: What are the key things that they'll have to think through next? What are going to be the key challenges? Who are the people they're going to need to influence next? By helping them think forward about what's coming as opposed to what's in the current moment, it helps them prepare and make decisions on their own toward the project, instead of looking for your individual direction in everything that they're doing.

Create Individual Development Plans

Collaborate with employees or mentees to create individual development plans with them. Have regular follow-up conversations, and assess their progress. Use the Exhausted Hero Model to identify what role they currently play and what role they wish to play in the future. In coaching, when we're thinking about a task or a project, we're trying not to be task focused; we're trying to be more big picture. It's the same thing with development. Instead of providing an individual's feedback around every little thing they're doing, how can we be more proactive in that feedback and say, "What are the things that you need to continue to work on? What are the behaviors that we need to see you continue to display? How are we focused on developing this over the next six months?" Help them build a development plan that can be executed together.

Schedule Time to Get out of Your Office

I have a client who conducts his one-on-one meetings with individual team members while taking a walk with the team member around the neighborhood of their offices. Why? Fresh air, movement, and sunshine are conducive to relaxed conversation and creativity—plus, it helps him keep focused on asking questions as opposed to getting too tactical. It is difficult to get too tactical when there isn't an agenda or a project plan in front of him. It creates a more open space for them to talk because it changes the dynamic; walking side by side shows that you're in there with them as opposed to over them.

Implement an Informal Recognition Program

Being an effective coach requires you to be an encourager, and not everyone is good at that. That's where an informal recognition program can come in handy. Back in my retail days, the district managers would go and visit stores; unfortunately, a few of these district managers got in the habit of being consistently critical. District managers started carrying five thank-you cards in their back pockets. When they witnessed a team member doing something great, they would stop and write them a thank-you card. Their goal was to fill out all five thank-you cards before they left the store. It was a way to hold themselves accountable for giving recognition to others.

How do you create recognition on a larger scale? When I ran the talent team at Sports Authority, we had a weekly Monday morning meeting. Part of the meeting was a thank-you session, in which we'd recognize good work from people on the team the preceding week. It kicked off the week on a positive note and reminded us all that we were there to help and support each other.

When Giving Feedback, Start with the Good News

There are a lot of different ways that people need to get feedback, both positive and negative. How do you get into a pattern of doing that? For me, I've had coaching clients who have added a feedback section to the top of every one of their one-on-one agendas. By starting the meeting with feedback, it ensured that feedback was covered in the meeting. And by starting with feedback, it was much easier to start with something positive. Then, the manager would add constructive feedback as well.

Take the Time to Get to Know Your Team

It's crucial to find out what is important to your team, both on the job and outside of the work environment. Take them to lunch or coffee, go sit outside, or just go for a walk. As you coach your team, you need to learn what motivates them. You need to know what inspires them. You need to know what causes them stress. This information helps to understand how to coach better and to figure out what inspires and motivates them to continue to develop and change. I coached a senior vice president who took each team member out to lunch and then would come back to the office to write a full page about what he'd learned about that person. It really helped him improve his listening skills too.

Practice Constructive-Feedback Conversations with a Peer before Having the Actual Conversation

Coaching can be an intimidating thing. Providing feedback or helping somebody think about the next step within their project can be difficult, but you can practice that. Take time to write what you plan to say. Detail the behaviors observed and the guidance to improve for next time. Sit down with a peer, a supervisor, or an executive coach and say, "I need to rehearse this conversation. Can we practice?" Going through what you're going to say out loud makes it easier to do, and you can get constructive feedback too.

Read *The Coaching Habit,* by Michael Bungay Stanier

This is a terrific book that will help you learn to coach and develop your team. It will help you get out of the directive and into empowering individuals to move forward and develop themselves, develop their projects, and develop their results.

Coaching is a habit. Once a manager becomes good at it, coaching becomes a natural conversation between a manager and direct report. It opens up trust, empowerment, fulfillment, and strategic capabilities.

DELEGATION SKILL DEVELOPMENT

Exhausted Heroes typically have a problem with delegating. Their challenge is getting to a place where the majority of the work within the team is pushed to the team, not back onto the leader. I'd estimate that out of all the executive coaching time that I've completed, more than 50 percent of it has been spent on learning how to delegate.

It's not an easy thing to hand over the responsibility to drive results, because you probably got promoted by being really good at getting stuff done. Naturally, you just want to keep getting stuff done—however that isn't the role of a Strategic Manager. Strategic Managers are entrusted with leading the team to handle the work, to effectively communicate the vision of what needs to happen, and to be able to coach others about what needs to happen.

The following five ideas should help you to sharpen your delegating skills so you can lead.

Partner with Your Supervisor

Take some time to meet with your supervisor and identify current responsibilities that can be delegated to an employee or peer as a learning opportunity. Assist in monitoring progress and advising as needed. When an employee whom I was coaching was promoted, one of the exercises I had him do was to sit down with his supervisor and go through his new job description point by point. That resulted in the job description being revised, as they both saw that some of the work delegated to him really should have gone to his staff. Having that meeting created a partnership up front and helped them both to properly set their expectations regarding workload.

Review the Delegation Arrow, and Identify Where Each Team Member Is on the Scale

Where are your team members on the delegation arrow (figure 5.3 in chapter 5)? Can they research and report back? Can they action plan? Can they tell you what the next steps are? Wherever they are, start to work toward moving them to the next step on the right. As I've said in previous chapters, delegation doesn't have to be an all-or-nothing thing. Tasks can be broken into parts, and those parts can be delegated. Research, for instance, can be delegated. An action plan can be built based on what needs to happen. How much you delegate to a particular person comes down to their experience level, their prior successes, and how much you trust them. Consider where they are within the model, and look for ways of letting them take on more responsibility.

Read *The One Minute Manager Meets the Monkey*, by Kenneth Blanchard

This is the book every manager should read and the one I most frequently gift to others. If you have issues with delegating, it should be at the top of your list too.

Blanchard provides the reader with the tools, tips, and tricks to effectively delegate. His inspirational tales will motivate you to try his delegation models and effectively manage the monkeys on your team.

The book is about 130 pages long. I read it once a year to remind myself to delegate and not take everything on myself.

Create a Written Plan of Action

Implement a team project process that includes the project owner creating a one-page charter that defines the objective's scope, milestones, and owners in a project. The process should also include a document called a timing and action plan. This plan includes a step-by-step description of each task that needs to be completed for the project and the expected completion date of major milestone tasks. It is an excellent way to give employees stakes in a project and accountability. Having this team project process and these two documents enables the manager to follow up on the progress to the agreed-upon plan.

As your direct reports build the project documents, they will understand the purpose, which ties back to the vision, but they also will understand their responsibilities and timelines.

Create Captainships on Your Team

Delegate an entire project or process, not just the steps in the project or process. Then, help the captain create a one-page charter and timing of action for their project.

When I was leading a team at Sports Authority, I assigned a team member, Trevor, to be captain of new-team-member onboarding. If any team member joined our team, Trevor was responsible for building and executing the onboarding plan. Before that, I spent the majority of my time as a manager trying to navigate who was supposed to be doing what and when with new hires.

Trevor still utilized the team to help onboard each new team member. With Trevor creating a strategy around onboarding, I was able to have bigger-picture conversations with the team. Trevor created the project plan and the timing and action document. His ownership of the entire onboarding process was much more rewarding than owning just a few steps in the process.

KEEP YOUR LEADERSHIP GAME PLAN ALIVE

Moving from being an Exhausted Hero to a Strategic Manager doesn't happen without effort. It calls for intentional, proactive personal development. I highly encourage you to build a Leadership Game Plan and then share that Game Plan with your boss. Pull it out on a quarterly basis to see how you're doing, and continue to reevaluate where you are on the Exhausted Hero Model.

Again, don't try to eat the whole apple in a single bite; choose one or two of these behaviors to start out. Two of these changes will make a practical shift in how you look at your job and your responsibilities. The Leadership Game Plan will help you step back from the insupportable and unhappy role of the Exhausted Hero and elevate you to the Strategic Manager role.

CHAPTER 7

THE RESPONSIBILITY OF SENIOR LEADERSHIP

E very year, Gallup conducts employee engagement surveys across the world at organizations of various sizes, with the mission to provide feedback and information to senior executives on how to increase employee engagement, retain outstanding talent, and deliver on business objectives.

Gallup defines "engaged" workers as employees who are involved in, enthusiastic about, and committed to their work and workplaces. In 2018, Gallup reported that 34 percent of the workforce in the United States met the standard of "engaged." That's fewer than four in ten employees. The percentage who are "actively disengaged" workers who reported miserable work experiences was 13 percent.[2]

The remaining 53 percent of workers are classified as "not

---

2   Jim Harter, "Employee Engagement on the Rise in the U.S.," Gallup. com, August 26, 2018, https://news.gallup.com/poll/241649/employee-engagement-rise.aspx.

engaged," which is defined by Gallup as generally satisfied but not cognitively or emotionally connected to their work and workplace. They will usually show up to work and do the minimum required. If these stats don't depress you, I encourage you to read them again. If only 34 percent of our employees are actively excited about going to work and the other 66 percent are just showing up, there is huge opportunity for improvement.

If an organization can increase their employee engagement levels, it could result in more innovative ideas, higher employee retention, better customer service, and decreased expenses from fixing mistakes or hiring new employees.

I think a great place to start is by ensuring organizations aren't exhausted. In this chapter, I'll speak to ways for senior leadership to increase the engagement of leaders across their organizations by eliminating Exhausted Heroes and creating Strategic Managers who will drive engagement throughout the rest of the organization.

SUPPORT LEADERSHIP GAME PLANS

A major responsibility of a senior leader is to support their Exhausted Heroes with Leadership Game Plans. As discussed in the previous chapter, these plans provide the road map from Exhausted Hero to Strategic Manager. But direct reports need support from their bosses through feedback, encouragement, and accountability.

In the hustle and bustle of an Exhausted Hero's schedule, they often lose sight of their priorities. This includes their own development. A senior leader can help them elevate their development to high priority.

A senior leader also can support a Leadership Game Plan by providing permission to try new approaches, learn new behaviors, and sometimes fail trying. An Exhausted Hero is often on edge trying to achieve and drive results. The boss can remind the Exhausted Hero that they are allowed to try new ways in order to grow and develop into a Strategic Manager.

The support of an Exhausted Hero's boss is critical to rescuing this important talent from themselves.

CREATE A STRATEGIC CULTURE

Are your leaders constantly putting out fires? Are they looking tired? Are they working long hours, while their teams magically leave work at 4:59 p.m. every day?

Is the business transforming and moving fast—so fast that people seem to always be running to catch up?

If this is the case, you may have an exhausted culture. And it is senior leadership's role to lead the transformation of an exhausted culture into a strategic culture.

A strategic culture is mobilized with a clear vision that everyone is aligned to achieve. The organization includes Visionary Leaders and Strategic Managers who are respected and

It is senior leadership's role to lead the transformation of an exhausted culture into a strategic culture. A strategic culture is mobilized with a clear vision that everyone is aligned to achieve.

are respectful to their team. The organization thrives in change by establishing clear projects and clear expectations. The fear to bring innovation and change is not welcome in a strategic culture.

See Something, Say Something

It starts with "see something, say something." I know what you are thinking: that this term is being used out of its usual context. After several school shootings in the United States, we began asking students that if they see or hear something out of the ordinary, to be brave enough to step up and say something, to create a safer school environment. I am asking executives that if they see someone who's exhausted or hear someone who's exhausted, they should be brave enough to step up and say something, to create a more strategic culture at work.

Remember Amanda? She quit because she was exhausted. Her boss and other senior leaders could have seen that she was working late, seemed consistently out of balance, was doing most of the work herself, and was starting to seem more tactical than strategic in her efforts. But no one stepped in to help. Instead, their indifference forced her to keep going and keep working as an Exhausted Hero.

Be the leader to "see something, say something"! It could be as simple and straightforward as, "You seem exhausted; are you OK?" Then use wisdom and experience to help them be less exhausted. Help them learn to delegate, encourage them to prioritize, and give them permission to find balance.

Be a Strategic Role Model

It is hard to "see something, say something" if the leader is an Exhausted Hero themselves. And if senior leadership is exhausted, then the culture is exhausted.

Tony Schwartz, CEO of the Energy Project, and Christine Porath, a professor of management at Georgetown University, wrote an article entitled "Your Boss's Work-Life Balance Matters as Much as Your Own."[3] They reference a study conducted in partnership with the *Harvard Business Review* surveying nineteen thousand employees. Only 25 percent reported that their leaders model sustainable work practices. I read that as 75 percent of leaders *aren't* demonstrating work-life balance.

More interestingly, Swartz and Porath studied those employees who said their leaders did model sustainable work practices. Those employees were 55 percent more engaged, ranked 72 percent higher in health and well-being, and were 77 percent more satisfied at work.

The culture of the company isn't about a mission statement or company values on a poster. It is about how we actually work, and that starts with the example set by the senior leaders at the top and every layer of leadership in between.

If a leader leads the team as a Visionary or a Strategic Manager, it is that much more unlikely that the team will become Exhausted Heroes.

Support Coaching and Leadership Development

When a teenager turns sixteen, we don't hand them the car keys and say, "You have been riding in a car for sixteen years, and you have been watching me drive. You must already know how to drive. Congratulations!" Can you imagine how that would play out?

So why, when we promote an individual contributor to manager, do we often say, "You have been on the team for a while, and you've reported to a manager. So here are five direct reports. Good luck!" Of course, they will struggle to figure it out. Just like a teenager learning

---

3   Tony Schwartz and Christine Porath, "Your Boss's Work-Life Balance
     Matters as Much as Your Own," *Harvard Business Review*, July 10, 2014,
     https://hbr.org/2014/07/your-bosss-work-life-balance-matters-as-much-
     as-your-own.

about how to use the gas pedal, the turn signals, and their mirrors, a new manager is learning to manage their team, manage projects, and manage resources.

As they continue to grow and develop, it is challenging to learn to create a clear vision, coach the team, and influence change. It is difficult to learn how to delegate work that you know how to do. And if it is difficult to do these things, it is even more difficult to train someone else to do these things. I encourage senior leaders to have a voice in supporting the use of executive coaching and leadership development programs.

Executive coaching provides the outside perspective that can help leaders overcome exhaustion and elevate to being strategic. It is often seen as an expense, not an investment. Be a voice in supporting this important resource in elevating leadership, retaining great talent, and defeating a culture of exhaustion.

A leadership development program can create a cohort of change champions to transform the culture. I once led a leadership program at a large national retailer that included a cohort of thirty leaders from across the business. Their biggest revelation after completing the program was the need to be proactive instead of reactive. They wanted a culture of strategy versus a culture of exhaustion. The group went to the senior leadership team to highly recommend, if not demand, that every leader take the program, including the senior leadership team. The CEO was so moved by their demand that he asked my learning and development team to take the executive leadership team through the program first. This ignited major

Don't let programs like executive coaching and leadership development be overlooked. Let them help to create a culture of strategy.

change in the organization, inspiring more self-awareness and creating more strategic leaders.

Don't let programs like executive coaching and leadership development be overlooked. Let them help to create a culture of strategy.

Design the Organization to Guard against Creating Exhausted Heroes

As I have worked with several organizations overwhelmed with too many Exhausted Heroes in their workforce, we often focus on the design of their organization. A common mistake that organizations make when designing their teams is creating manager positions with only one direct report.

If a manager is given only one direct report, then that manager needs to be a Working Manager. They can't delegate everything to one person, so they will need to step in and help. The manager is often pushed into an Exhausted Hero role when their supervisor also demands that they become a strategic leader, forcing them to take on leadership while being a manager and an individual contributor.

If the organization is designed for the manager to only have one direct report, the manager's boss will need to carry the load for creating a vision and influencing change.

A trend over the last few decades is continuing to flatten organizations by eliminating layers of middle managers. This allows for less confusion around decision responsibilities and decreases bureaucracy. I think flattening organizations can also help eliminate Exhausted Heroes, if the remaining managers become Strategic Managers and not Working Managers. A flat organization typically results in more direct reports per manager, enabling the Strategic Manager to delegate while having time to perform the leader-focused behaviors.

Hire Strategic Managers from the Start

Senior leadership must develop Strategic Managers and encourage an environment in which they flourish. This starts with recruiting and hiring. Many hiring managers unintentionally design roles that ultimately create Exhausted Heroes. Or they assign new hires a set of responsibilities that make them Exhausted Heroes from day one.

Strategic Managers are experienced enough to recognize when this happens and push back. But Working Managers, on the other hand, may accept an Exhausted Hero role, not knowing better. It's up to senior leadership to know better.

In many cases, senior leadership thinks they need a different kind of manager than they actually do. In most cases I've seen, senior leadership focuses on hiring a manager who is considered a technical expert, when they'd be much better served by a Strategic Manager experienced in leading teams.

I was recently consulting in a large government agency. As I was attempting to analyze the teams' needs, I asked employees what makes a great leader in this organization. I found it amazing how important "technical expertise" was perceived to be. I was told, "They know all the processes and procedures this part of the agency completes, and they know the policies and the laws." The answer to what made a great leader seemed to be "everything technical."

For this governmental agency, the value placed on technical expertise stemmed from the executive leadership team, who were all strong technical or functional experts.

Because the top was so focused on technical expertise, the number one thing other leaders were hired for was technical expertise. They weren't looking for leaders. Everybody could do the work, but nobody could explain or direct what work to do. Nobody could tell anyone what work was going to be important down the road. Exhausted Heroes weren't thinking ahead, because they were just thinking about what they needed to do today.

When interviewing and recruiting, we must ask ourselves, "What does somebody need to have to be a director? Or a VP? Or an executive vice president?" Most look for experience in operations, or in finance, or in marketing. Then they describe a list of technical experience requirements, like "need to have managed a large P&L," and the description ends there.

We are missing a huge opportunity if we don't hire someone with experience in the four big-ticket items that make a successful Strategic Manager:

1. Create a vision.

2. Influence change.

3. Coach others.

4. Delegate.

We must prioritize these four qualities when we interview candidates. The key question is no longer, "Do they know how to technically make us more money, technically improve this product, or technically drive the sales organization?"

The most important question is "Do they know how to lead?"

The most important question is "Do they know how to lead?"

SENIOR LEADERS, AVOID THESE EXHAUSTION TRAPS

Now that you know how to support a strategic culture, know how to elevate an individual manager with a Game Plan, and know how to hire all future managers to be Strategic Managers, what are some traps that need to be avoided?

1. Don't forget about the individual.

2. Don't delegate your role as a supervisor.

3. Don't wait for the company culture to change your culture.

4. Don't allow overcommitment.

5. Don't forget to listen.

1. Don't Forget about the Individual

The supervisor is the most important person who contributes to an employee's development, aside from the employee themselves. Yet many supervisors don't realize the significance of their role. I've worked with supervisors who are capable managers, or enthusiastic team leaders, or technical experts—but what many lack is understanding of the 1:1 nature of their role, and what it means to invest in the direct report's development as an *individual*.

The actual role of supervisor includes a sphere of responsibility that many supervisors aren't aware of. Most think, "I'll do the reviews and make the reports for our progress, and just make sure our team's on track and hitting our numbers." However, if a supervisor ignores their responsibility to assist in their direct reports' professional development, then a void is created in both the development of the employee and the effectiveness of the team in delivering results.

I was talking to a managing partner who'd recently been assigned a new boss. After about three months, he said to this boss: "I'm not getting a lot of feedback. I'd love to hear your perspective on my performance."

The boss replied, "Well, I don't get feedback from my boss, so I don't know how to give that to you."

Unfortunately, if one supervisor isn't involved in and responsible for their direct reports' professional development, a chain effect is created. Don't assume that on-the-job development or off-site activities and programs can replace the role of supervisor. Make time for one-on-one check-ins with your team. Take time to provide guidance, and coach the individual to better use their strengths. Help them to build an individual Game Plan for success.

> **Take time to provide guidance, and coach the individual to better use their strengths. Help them to build an individual Game Plan for success.**

2. Don't Delegate Your Role as a Supervisor

When they're looking to develop their high-potential talent, many executives will hire an external coach or someone to build a high-potential program so they can simply check "develop my team" off their to-do list.

There is a benefit to external coaching and workshops. But on the job, how they actually complete their work is the responsibility of their supervisor—and it always will be. The *supervision* part of supervising has more of an impact on learning than even an executive coach or a leadership program can have. Together, these initiatives and perspectives integrate into a plan that ensures an individual elevates successfully.

Yes, hiring an executive coach provides needed support to the direct report. Yes, it's essential to have a leadership program that helps teach new leadership skills. But it is the responsibility of the individual and their supervisor to implement these learnings on the job for practical purposes. This partnership—and sponsorship—from the executive team is helping them on a day-to-day basis, giving them feedback and reinforcement to help them be successful.

The reality is this: outside coaching can only get Exhausted Heroes so far. A supervisor can't delegate their role as a supervisor. At the end of the day, leaders must continue to coach Exhausted Heroes as well.

3. Don't Wait for the Company Culture to Change *Your* Culture

The third trap many supervisors fall into is waiting for the CEO or HR to change the company culture to support Strategic Managers. When it comes to developing the culture of the team, a leader doesn't need to wait for permission from the CEO. The CEO doesn't have to push this approach from the top down. Leaders can just get started with their own team and direct report(s).

In every industry across corporate America, I am noticing a trend of people being too paralyzed to move or to take action, because they're waiting for a cue from the CEO.

Having clear expectations is about the manager and their direct report—the CEO doesn't factor into the equation. Middle managers can't control everyone, least of all the CEO. And they can't reasonably be responsible for changing the culture of the entire company. But managers can control the conversations with direct reports. Managers can set the culture of the team and encourage more strategic planned work instead of exhausting firefighting work.

4. Don't Allow Overcommitment

Overcommitment also comes from being that type A personality who wants to achieve it all ... now! It is easy to see all the challenges that need to be met, but it is more difficult to prioritize and schedule those challenges. We all want to be able to do it all, but sometimes we need to commit to what can actually be accomplished with the time, resources, and quality available. And as supervisors, we need to help our teams to determine reasonable commitments.

Being overcommitted can limit a manager's strategic viewpoint. If a manager is so focused on what needs to happen today, then all of a sudden, a blind spot appears, preventing the leader from seeing potential future roadblocks. What challenges are coming next? What does the end product need to be? Prepare for the future by planning forward, talking with the team, researching, and networking.

Planning takes time and involves asking a lot of questions to determine future challenges. This is not something to do in one's free time.

Many of us say yes when we shouldn't. Saying yes overcommits us and often contributes to exhaustion. Rather than saying yes or no, there's a third option: "Yes, and ... " followed by you asking for whatever support you need to accomplish the request. Kelly Leonard and Tom Yorton wrote the book *Yes, And* based on their experience in the world of improv comedy, where the phrase "Yes, and ... " is a way to keep the skit going with creativity and collaboration.

When a Strategic Manager agrees to a work request, how does the Strategic Manager *not* just sign up and make themselves the Exhausted Hero? How do they sign up and make themselves the leader? Try to use this phrase: "Yes, and ... "

Here are examples:

- Yes, I think we need to do that, and I think I can get that done by June of next year.

- Yes, we need to do that, and I need additional resources to make that happen.

- Yes, I think we can do that, and it may take a few drafts to get it right.

The strategic answer of "Yes, and ... " is much more powerful. It provides the leader with the ability to support the commitments of the company and gain the time and resources to appropriately complete the task. It allows the leader to avoid being overcommitted and exhausted.

5. Don't Forget to Listen

The team often knows how to avoid exhaustion—sometimes the manager just needs to listen to them to realize it.

Not listening to the needs of the team is one way to create challenges that escalate into a culture of exhaustion. If the manager is sensing exhaustion, the best thing they can do is pull the team in and ask, "What's going on? What's happening? What are you nervous about? What do we do to solve this?" Bring them in and encourage them to become part of the solution.

And when listening to the team, use the third dimension of listening. In the book *Co-active Coaching*, Level III listening is described as "Global Listening." This is when you listen not just to what's being said in a meeting but also to the mood of the room, the energy of the person talking, and the environment or culture. In this case, do you feel the exhaustion as you have this discussion? Listen for signs of fear or energy that resemble exhaustion, or for a mood of defeat. Level III Global Listening is a great skill for leaders helping their teams to avoid exhaustion.

THE RESPONSIBILITY WE SHARE FOR EXHAUSTION

As I stated throughout this book, building Strategic Managers and eliminating Exhausted Heroes are the responsibilities of both the individual leader and the senior leaders of the organization.

In the workplace, it's common for everybody to look at somebody else to solve any given challenge. Stop pointing fingers, and start working together to solve the problem!

Many senior leaders may have had a mentor or boss help develop them from Exhausted Heroes into Strategic Managers. And many wish they would have had that mentor or boss. Either way, pay it forward and support your Exhausted Hero. Work together to build a strategic culture with the team.

CHAPTER 8

THE ROLE OF LEADERSHIP DEVELOPMENT

"Y ou have been a great individual contributor. Now you are a manager, so here are five direct reports—don't screw them up."

When I share this sentence with leaders across corporate America, they almost always smile in recognition and admit that this is the state of leadership development in most organizations.

If we are going to rescue Corporate Exhausted Heroes and save the culture of work in America from being about exhaustion, we need our good managers to be developed intentionally, through coaching, education, and a gradual introduction to increased responsibility. If we fail to prepare them to handle their new assignments, we can't be surprised if they fail.

Let's build intentional development programs that prepare them for success and enable them to drive the results on which we all depend.

BE INTENTIONAL

Regardless of which kind of leadership development strategy is being implemented, the critical point is that it be intentional, not haphazard, and that it create a consistency across the board for rising managers.

> We need our good managers to be developed intentionally, through coaching, education, and a gradual introduction to increased responsibility. If we fail to prepare them to handle their new assignments, we can't be surprised if they fail.

Simply promoting a promising person into a leadership role without adequate preparation is a recipe for creating Exhausted Heroes and muddying the waters around your company's specific culture and expectations. Just giving a stand-alone workshop won't solve that problem; that's not enough to drive the results and desired outcomes.

New managers need not only to learn the tips, tricks, and skills to do their jobs; they also need to learn behaviors, reset their own expectations around what they should and shouldn't do, and be provided with ongoing support and collaboration in order to succeed.

In my observations, and as evidenced by countless studies, it is the intentional blend of many modes of learning that works best. Within the most successful and effective leadership development programs for high-potential employees, they include cohort-based workshops. They have formal coaching in between workshops, and then they also have on-the-job assignments, where they take something they've learned from the workshop and immediately implement it back on the job. Participants have accountability partners to help support each other in learning and practice. This kind of blended learning approach is what makes leadership development impactful—not just workshops, not just real-world experience, not just assignments, not just having the input of a mentor, but all of these in combination.

FOUR LEVELS OF LEADERSHIP DEVELOPMENT

There are four levels of investment that an organization can implement in developing their future leaders. If companies are looking for strong results from their management teams, these four levels of leadership development provide options to best fit the organizations' needs based on their ability to invest.

Which level will best support an organization in developing Strategic Managers? It really depends on the size of the organization, the size of the leadership team, the dedicated resources focused on leadership development, and the level of financial investment available to support these essential leaders. As you review the four levels of leadership development, identify the method that works best for you and your organization.

Level IV: Integrated Leadership Development System

This program represents the best and most comprehensive leadership development program. This system integrates the majority of the leadership development best practices.

Massive corporations know how important proper preparation is for success in leadership, so they put together comprehensive programs that consistently prepare their team members for the next level, starting all the way back at onboarding new hires. Through large cohorts of those being promoted or the newly hired learning together, these often lengthy and multifaceted processes can take many forms. The ultimate goal is to teach, mentor, and prepare the person for the new responsibilities they're taking on. These programs continue as leaders move up the corporate ladder, assisting them at each rung or promotion with intentional development.

These kinds of programs require a significant investment of money and time, so they aren't always within the reach of smaller and middle-sized enterprises. General Electric's legendary former CEO Jack Welch was a big proponent of training programs for both new hires and leaders within the organization. Under his leadership, GE created innovative and effective training programs. GE built several levels of leadership development programs through their Crotonville, New York, leadership retreat center. Across this large organization, leaders were identified for their potential for an upcoming promotion to a new leadership level. They then attended retreats and participated in month- and year-long programs to prepare them to be a manager, a director, a vice president, or a senior executive. Jack Welch created a talent management supply chain that built an engineered process to develop leaders from the moment they entered the company. This method was copied across large *Fortune* 500 companies globally.

I experienced this program through Target Corporation, and it is a great example of how a big company does it right. When I graduated from Indiana University with my business degree, I had the good fortune to be hired by the Target Corporation as a business analyst. At that point there were about nine thousand employees working at the Minneapolis headquarters, and about nine hundred stores nationwide.

As soon as I'd been hired, I was enrolled in a sixteen-week merchandising training program with sixteen other recent college graduates, which was the Target way to onboard new hires. First, we learned how to do our jobs—the theoretical concepts, the computer systems we used, and the processes of the organization. Then, we were spread out across the different departments. Mine was healthcare, and like the other trainees, I was paired with a mentor to train me. They'd review how we were doing in class and step in to help us out when we weren't catching on—"You just finished the training course on reporting. Let's go pull some reports together"—and we'd learn on the job. Not only did we have a mentor guiding us who knew the job, but we also had a manager to oversee our training experience and make sure we were getting what we needed. The whole process was beautifully organized and completely intentional.

But it was only the start of my development as a leader. From day one, Target started me on the talent management supply chain process to make me into a senior executive someday.

When I was promoted to the next level—the Rockstar role—I also took on a mentoring role, training new hires as I'd been trained. This next step in the leadership development process was intentionally preparing me to become a Working Manager.

Before I was promoted to my first manager role, Target enrolled me in a ten-week training program in which I was taught how to manage work, how to give feedback to others, how to recognize and inspire others, and very importantly, how my role changed from being a doer to managing doers. I was taught that my job wasn't to take on everyone's tasks myself—it was managing others who were tasked with getting specific things done and staying on top of their progress toward project goals. They taught me to be a Working Manager.

Target continued their supply chain for talent with unique programs to help talent elevate to the next levels: director, vice president, and senior executive.

Target's well-designed system supplied education and support where it was needed and enabled me and others to move up to greater responsibility while avoiding the pitfalls that lead to becoming an Exhausted Hero. Every level of the supply chain for leadership development included cohort-based learning opportunities that were several months long and included workshops, mentorships, coaching, and on-the-job practice.

A Level IV Integrated Leadership Development System is the highest level of intensity and intentionality that a company can invest into developing their future leaders.

A Level IV Integrated Leadership Development System is the highest level of intensity and intentionality that a company can invest into developing their future leaders. It requires commitment, an internal leadership development team, and significant financial resources. I encourage large companies to consider implementing this very important leadership development system that will produce a high rate of return on investment with the future leaders of the organization. If the organization is not large enough to invest in this system, there are three other levels of leadership development that should be considered.

Level III: The Company High-Potential Program Model

In contrast to an integrated systematic approach, this program focuses on the key level within your organization where leadership truly rises to the Strategic Manager role. These programs are focused on elevating Exhausted Heroes and Working Managers to the Strategic Manager role.

These high-potential leadership development programs are cohort-driven development programs in which leaders work together toward a common goal. From a facilitator's point of view, the sweet spot for participants in a group is sixteen to twenty individuals at a time. These are all managers and leaders at similar levels who are experiencing similar transitions within their leadership roles. By learning together as a cohort, a powerful support system is created for those who are going through these changes together.

An example program I designed with peers at Red Robin Gourmet Burgers was called the School of Leadership. The organization had identified vice presidents and directors who were highly successful in their roles and invested in this program to assist them in becoming better Strategic Managers. The program included three retreats that were each a week in length, conducted about two months apart.

At the first retreat, we focused on self-leadership. We used assessments among other tools to identify their strengths so we could figure out how to maximize those strengths to the greatest possible extent. Then, participants went back to their jobs, where they were tasked with implementing the skills and behaviors that they had learned.

Two months later, the participants returned for the second retreat, where they learned about communication, delegation, project management, and other skills that helped manage their teams more effectively. Returning to the job, they had to implement things like better one-on-ones, more productive team meetings, and more effective project plans to drive greater results.

Finally, participants came back for their final retreat, which was about organizational leadership. The sixteen leaders learned how to influence change, how to create a vision for the team, and how to coach and motivate others.

Over the six months of the high-potential leadership development program, these leaders grew into Strategic Managers. We received feedback from their teams that their leadership had improved through better communication, enhanced planning, and an openness to new and better strategies. The senior leaders in the organization gained new trust in these leaders and asked them to lead larger projects that had a higher impact on the success of the company. This intentional, focused, and well-constructed program created the future leaders of the organization.

A Level III high-potential program works at the majority of organizations, but not all companies are ready for this program. Many companies need to first define what is expected of leaders. For these, the next level of leadership development might be a better option.

Level II: The Company Leadership Expectation Program Model

I was working with a national franchise business in Denver recently; they'd never really talked to their team about their expectations for leaders in the organization. The company was growing, and many leaders were Exhausted Heroes.

We worked together to establish a Company Leadership Expectation Program focused on defining and teaching a new set of expectations and skills they wanted all of their managers and leaders to follow.

The first step in creating a Company Leadership Expectation Program was sitting down with the leadership team and presenting them with a list of topics and behaviors, and then asking which of those behaviors they really wanted to see elevated within the organization. Out of many possible choices, we identified six topics— among them influencing others, creating a vision, communicating effectively, and coaching, the main leadership behaviors of Strategic

Managers. I developed workshops around each desired behavior, not only to give tips or build skills but also to clearly define what was expected of the leaders within that organization.

For this particular organization, I facilitated a unique workshop once every month for ninety minutes. These were highly interactive and covered multiple leadership models. They helped their team to understand the company's definition of and expectations for leadership, to have conversations around those expectations, and to understand how they could be applied to the individual's management style.

Not only did it help them create the desired leadership behaviors, but because it was cohort driven, it also helped people see beyond their silos and increased collaboration among different divisions across the company. Managers have a lot of the same challenges—influencing upper management, influencing down, providing feedback, delegating—all things that many managers struggle with, no matter what department they're in. That meant that these managers who had previously felt isolated now had a connection to peers who were experiencing very similar challenges.

Level I: One-on-One Executive Coaching

As I mentioned, programs that have high scope and scale aren't always appropriate or even possible in smaller enterprises. Executive coaching provides a great substitute for those programs because it's one-on-one. It gives the individual the support they need to make the transition from being a Working Manager to becoming a Strategic Manager.

Executive coaching is also particularly important when you get to senior levels within an organization, because many people at that level don't really have peers. So it's tough to design and conduct a workshop when there are only three or four high-level individuals moving from Strategic Manager to the Visionary stage of leadership.

One-on-one executive coaching is a great way to give the individual the development they need to be able to move up to the next level. This kind of coaching may be brought on board via the HR department, by the executives themselves, or by their bosses.

The choice to employ executive coaching doesn't necessarily have to be tied to a promotion. We see executive coaching being launched both on a proactive and a reactive basis. A proactive basis is the more positive approach: a coach is brought in to help someone who's poised to move up soon within the organization. That leader's been identified as having the potential to rise to another level, so coaching is provided to help them develop needed skills and behaviors that will get them prepared for that set of challenges.

From a reactive standpoint, the thinking might be, "They've transitioned to a new level, but they're just missing something." A specific weakness is identified where improvement is needed to ensure success in the more demanding position. Often, I'm brought in as an executive coach to help teach that new behavior, to help them figure out the barrier that's preventing them from employing that behavior, and to help prepare them to make that next-level transition. In either scenario, executive coaching is a smart investment. Clearly, the better prepared the rising star is for that bigger job, the more likely they are to thrive in it.

Often leaders aren't initially comfortable with the idea of coaching. The attitude I tend to hear is, "Isn't that all a little touchy-feely?" A study by the International Coach Foundation says otherwise: coaching was rated as "profoundly beneficial" by those companies and individuals who hired coaches, with 99 percent rating themselves as satisfied or very satisfied with the outcome and 96 percent stating that they would repeat the process again.[4]

The fact is, coaching is an organized process structured to help the individual dig in, determine their strengths, and work through the challenges they currently face in order to use those strengths to their best advantage.

KEEP IT INTENTIONAL

Regardless of which level of leadership development strategy is right for a particular organization's needs, the critical point here is the solution should be intentional.

> Coaching is an organized process structured to help the individual dig in, determine their strengths, and work through the challenges they currently face in order to use those strengths to their best advantage.

An Exhausted Hero can and should be rescued. They can rescue themselves by building a Leadership Game Plan and developing new leader behaviors, intentionally. They can be rescued by a boss, who can support their Leadership Game Plan to elevate to Strategic Manager, intentionally. And Exhausted Heroes can participate in leadership development programs that are built to develop the future leaders of the company, intentionally.

The options are present. The choice is yours. Let's start the journey away from being exhausted.

---

4   "IFC Global Coaching Client Study," International Coach Federation, 2009.

DON'T LOOK FOR ANOTHER SUPERHERO TO COME TO YOUR RESCUE

E ven though Superman or Wonder Woman won't be swooping down to rescue you, you *can* save yourself from becoming (or continuing to be) an Exhausted Hero. Picking up this book was a great first step toward that end, and hopefully it has set you on a healthier path. Now you have some tactics and some guidelines on how to change.

As I reflect on Amanda's story from chapter 1, I am reminded of Amanda's thoughts while eating the piece of cake in the coffee shop. After just resigning, she wondered how she—and her senior leadership—could have done things differently to avoid becoming an Exhausted Hero. Well, I spoke to her recently. Amanda has learned to develop her leader-focused behaviors, learned to have brave conversations with her manager, and now is a senior leader of an organization focused on building a strategic culture.

As I ride the train into downtown Denver each Monday morning, I see many executives who look exhausted, just like Amanda did. As I ride up the elevator of a high-rise, I see more exhaustion. Exhaustion is taking over corporate America, and it is time to pause. It is time to rethink how we are going about the duty of work.

We can achieve it all without doing it all. We just need to do it smarter than we are doing it today.

OVERCOMING EXHAUSTION IS POSSIBLE

You never fail, until you stop trying.

—*Albert Einstein*

Don't give up. Don't lose hope. Just try to do it in a different way.

These highly successful leaders exist! I know them!

- A CEO who makes it home for dinner with the family 90 percent of the time, and whose corporation continues to increase revenue

- A director who takes a lunch break every single day and continues to build new business models and processes for the company

- A sales professional who puts her phone in a drawer after five o'clock and still consistently blows away her sales goals

- A vice president who volunteers at his child's school once a quarter and still earns his annual bonus

- An entrepreneur who goes to the gym five days a week and still has the energy to lead her company to new, innovative endeavors

When I tell Corporate Exhausted Heroes about these people, they either think I am talking about superheroes with special powers, or they say, "Yes, but my job is different." My answer is, "No, these leaders' jobs aren't any easier. They just chose to be a different kind of leader." They are leaders who have chosen to lead instead of being led. They are leaders who have chosen to work with others instead of going it alone. They are leaders who have chosen to be strategic instead of being exhausted. They are leaders who are achieving it all, without doing it all themselves.

CHOOSE TO BE STRATEGIC

I hope you have found several ways you can choose to be a Strategic Manager or a Visionary Leader instead of a Corporate Exhausted Hero. It is really that simple: choose to be strategic.

I have coached countless Exhausted Heroes who have worked eighty hours a week, given up on all health goals, struggled through stressful home lives, and asked me to help rescue them from their horrible world of stress. Through discovery, we often determine that the only person who is holding them hostage is themselves. Rarely is there an evil villain playing the part of the boss who chains the Exhausted Hero to their desk. Rarely is this evil boss monitoring their Exhausted Hero's hours, watching to see if they take a lunch, and demanding the effort that the Exhausted Hero is producing. Through coaching and development, I have rescued Exhausted Heroes from themselves and assisted them in building new leadership skills that elevate them to Strategic Managers.

Choose to be strategic. Make choices like those suggested in the chapters of this book to elevate your leadership. It isn't about choosing to achieve less; it's about achieving the same, if not more, by doing it better, smarter, and more strategically. Don't wait to be saved—choose a new strategic path now!

CREATE A STRATEGIC CULTURE

My biggest wish in writing this book is to create awareness of exhaustion in the corporate workplace. The pandemic of exhaustion is unacceptable. I have asked several supervisors about their direct reports' exhausting habits, and most say, "That is just who they are." I politely ask you to reconsider your perspective! That is who you have let them become. It isn't that you trained them to be exhausted, but you haven't trained them to avoid exhaustion either.

Many human resource departments are focused on defining, reinventing, building, or elevating their corporate culture. Many are building snack bars, buying foosball tables, allowing more flexible work-from-home schedules, and creating on-site gyms. This isn't where to start. Let me give you a hint: start with exhaustion. Why are leaders exhausted? And why are leaders allowing their teams to be exhausted?

Cultures that aren't exhausted have a strong leadership development program for leaders at every level. They're made up of leaders who model balanced work and life, who invest in leadership coaching for their emerging leaders. Cultures that aren't exhausted are made up of teams who are focused on supporting collaboration and team management, instead of promoting individual heroism.

No one deserves a life sentence of exhaustion. It is my mission to eliminate exhaustion in the corporate world and build the next generation of great leaders. Together, we can rescue Exhausted Heroes and the companies that rely on them.

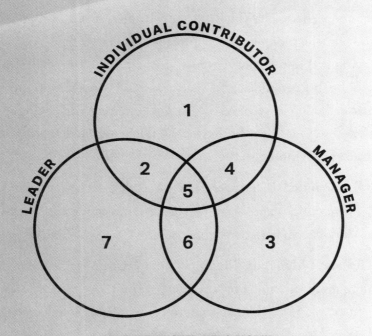

THE EXHAUSTED HERO MODEL

1. Taskmaster
2. Rockstar
3. Clipboard Manager
4. Working Manager
5. Exhausted Hero
6. Strategic Manager
7. Visionary

In many models of integration, the center represents the optimal result. In this Exhausted Hero Model, the center point, or Exhausted Hero (5), is the least optimal role.

1. **Taskmaster**. The Taskmaster is an individual contributor hired to get stuff done. Their scope is relatively small, they're focused mostly on short-term task lists, and there is often a lot of repetition in their work.

   - **Associated behaviors**: Drives results, serves as technical/functional expert, learns/teaches others

2. **Rockstar**. The Rockstar is the integration of individual-contributor and leader roles. The Rockstar continues to get stuff done but also starts working on larger projects, teaching others, and identifying and implementing more efficient and effective processes. In some organizations, this is a promotion. In others, it isn't. No matter how it is recognized, it's not rewarded with being given a team ... yet. But the Rockstar's leadership and focus on the future is beginning to show.

   - **Associated behaviors**: Drives results, serves as technical/functional expert, learns/teaches others, creates a vision, influences change, coaches others

3. **Clipboard Manager**: The Clipboard Manager has gained a team, more resources, and a broader scope. This person is paid to keep focused on today, the short term. Their focus is on managing the spinning plates. They're not tasked with adding more plates but with keeping those already spinning in motion. Clipboard Managers also drop all individual-contributor responsibilities through delegation.

   - **Associated behaviors**: Manages team, manages resources, manages projects

4. **Working Manager**: The Working Manager is the integration between individual contributor and manager. The Working

Manager manages a team but also gains or retains additional individual-contributor duties. Sometimes a Working Manager is a former Clipboard Manager who has gained the efficiencies and effectiveness of managing their team, so they can now take on additional individual-contributor responsibilities. Other Working Managers may manage a small team while having the ability to maintain individual-contributor roles in meeting the needs of the business.

- **Associated behaviors**: Drives results, serves as technical/functional expert, learns/teaches others, manages team, manages resources, manages projects

5. **Exhausted Hero**: This role includes maintaining responsibility for individual contributors' work and managing the team, while adding the requirement of looking forward by building a vision, leading change, and influencing the future of the department or team. In other words, it combines the roles of the individual contributor, manager, and leader. This role is overwhelming, and that often shows in both results and team health.

- **Associated behaviors**: Drives results, serves as technical/functional expert, learns/teaches others, manages team, manages resources, manages projects, creates a vision, influences change, coaches others

6. **Strategic Manager**: These leaders represent the integration between manager and leader roles. They focus on managing their teams and planning for the future, while delegating all individual-contributor work. This allows the Strategic Manager to lead by effectively setting the vision, influencing the future, and coaching the team to deliver results.

- **Associated behaviors**: Manages team, manages resources, manages projects, creates a vision, influences change, coaches others

7. **Visionary**: This leader is 100 percent focused on the future and delegates the day-to-day management of the vision to managers and their teams to drive. They also lead change, influence others, and coach their management team to make the vision come to life.

- **Associated behaviors**: Creates a vision, influences change, coaches others

Individual-Contributor-Focused Behaviors

- **Drives results**: Individual contributors deliver tasks to complete a project or process. They are responsible for completing these tasks or groups of tasks in a timely and effective process.

- **Has technical/functional expertise**: Individual contributors gain proficiency and sometimes mastery of their role through technical capabilities or mastering a procedure.

- **Learns and teaches others**: Coupled with technical/functional expertise, it is important for an individual contributor to be a learner and, as they achieve expertise, a teacher of others.

Manager-Focused Behaviors

- **Manages team**: Through recognition, feedback, advice, and managing accountabilities, the manager ensures their team of individual contributors is on track to achieve the team goals.

- **Manages resources**: Through managing budget, head count, assignments, timelines, and cross-functional support, managers ensure their team of individual contributors has the resources needed to achieve the team goals.

- **Manages projects**: Managers step above the tasks and oversee the group of tasks or projects. By managing the projects to drive accountability, managers ensure the team is set up for success.

Leader-Focused Behaviors

- **Creates a vision**: A leader needs to be the guide; they must establish the purpose, build the goals, and create a vision for the future. An effective leader creates clarity, inspiration, and success with this vision.

- **Influences change**: It is important that leaders keep the business changing, evolving, and elevating. An influential leader can lead an organization down a path to the vision. Influencing could be inspiring, persuading, or gaining partnership to enable the capabilities for success.

- **Coaches others**: A manager often leads from the back: "Go do this. Why didn't you do this?" A coach leads from the front: "Come this way. How can I help? What do you need?" A coach develops their team with new skills and provides opportunities through stretch assignments.

The Kubler-Ross Change Curve

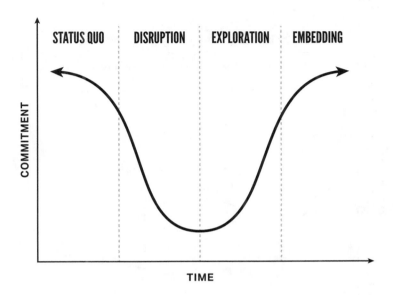

The Twenty-Minute Conversation and the Coaching Curve

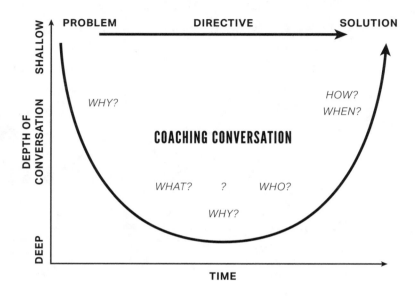

The coaching curve represents a twenty-minute conversation focused on coaching, not being directive. The conversation is deep, full of questions, and clarifies perspectives.

The Delegation Arrow

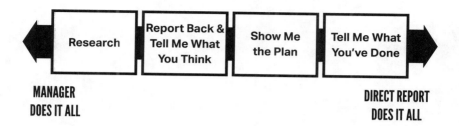

On the left end is the overcommitted manager who says, "Don't worry; I'll do it all." On the other end is the hands-off manager who says, "I don't even want to touch any of this; go do it," and just prays it gets done correctly. Neither strategy is good delegation.